Hippocrene Insiders' Guide to
POLAND'S JEWISH HERITAGE

D0062813

Hippocrene Insiders' Guide to
POLAND'S JEWISH HERITAGE

Joram Kagan

HIPPOCRENE BOOKS
New York

Copyright © 1992 by Joram Kagan

All rights reserved, including the right to reproduce this
book or portions thereof in any form.

For information, address:
Hippocrene Books, Inc.
171 Madison Avenue
New York NY 10016

Library of Congress Cataloging-in-Publication Data is
available.

ISBN 0-87052-991-9

Printed in the United States of America.

To the Righteous Few

CONTENTS

PREFACE

By and large both English and Polish names are used in this guide, i.e., Warsaw (Warszawa) etc., to facilitate location of places. Also "shetel" names are added as these were widely used by Jewish immigrants to the U.S.A., e.g., Tykocin is Tiktin. Spelling of names may show the Polish spelling, e.g. Sztajn or the English one, i.e. Shtein/Stein, depending on the sources of information. Some Hebrew names have been used, such as "Matzevot," "Ohel," "Tzadik," "Beth Madrash," "Shoah," etc., which often more accurately describe the subject.

To enable one to find streets, etc., Polish names are used:

Ulica = Street
Aleje = Avenue
Plac = Square

is only reasonable to expect that some names of streets, particularly those having the communist regime connotation, will be changed. At the present time the information on the subject is quite limited.

Limitations

Due to typographic limitations some typical Polish letters are shown only as English appoximates as follows:

ą = a
ć = c
ę = e
ń = n
ó = o
ś = s
ż = z
ź = z
ł = l

Whenever reference is made to the "War," unless otherwise stated, it means World War II.

ACKNOWLEDGMENTS

I wish to express my gratitude to Akiva Kohane and Paula Borenstein for their initial introduction to the "Jewish" Poland; to Monika Krajewska and Malgozata Niezabitowska, whose work on the Polish Jewry left a lasting impression on me; and to my friends Marian Turski, and Jerzy Tomaszewski, who in their knowledge of Polish-Jewish history have no peers.

My special thanks go to Dr. Simha Wajs, whose efforts to commemorate the Jewry of Lublin, my home town, are unique.

It was always a pleasure to see my friend Mordechai Palzur, whose hospitality during his term as Israel's ambassador to Poland was matchless.

I also wish to acknowledge assistance given to me during my 30 trips to Poland by my friends at Lot Polish Airlines.

I greatly appreciate the generous permission of Orbis to use their material and Henryk Grynberg to quote his magnificent poem "Poplars." Martin Gilbert's very kind permission to use his world famous maps permitted me to put some historical perspective to this work. I am confident it will make all the difference to the reader.

Last but not least I thank Marion Donnel and Sabina Franco for "suffering in silence" my numerous changes and additions to the manuscript, and specially Rafi Rothstein, as well as Sylvia Bruzzese, and Daphna Raz, whose encouragement was always most welcome.

There are, of course, many more individuals whom I met during my frequent trips to Poland and who always added some new dimension to my knowledge. They are too numerous to be all mentioned by name, but I thank them all.

MOURNER'S KADDISH

Yitgadal v'yitkadash sh'mei raba
b'alma di v'ra chirutei,
v'yamlich malchutei
b'cha-yeichon
uv-yomeichon, uv-cha-yei
d'chol bet Yisrael, ba'agala
u-vizman kariv, v'imru
Amein.

יִתְגַּדַּל וְיִתְקַדַּשׁ שְׁמֵהּ רַבָּא
בְּעָלְמָא דִּי בְרָא כִרְעוּתֵהּ,
וְיַמְלִיךְ מַלְכוּתֵהּ, בְּחַיֵּיכוֹן
וּבְיוֹמֵיכוֹן, וּבְחַיֵּי דְכָל־בֵּית
יִשְׂרָאֵל, בַּעֲגָלָא וּבִזְמַן קָרִיב,
וְאִמְרוּ אָמֵן.

Y'hei sh'mei raba m'vorach l'alam ul-almei almaya.

יְהֵא שְׁמֵהּ רַבָּא מְבָרַךְ לְעָלַם
וּלְעָלְמֵי עָלְמַיָּא.

Yitbarach v'yishtabach
v'yitpa'ar v'yitromam
v'yitnasei, v'yit-hadar
v'yitaleh v'yit-halal sh'mei
d'kudsha, b'rich Hu. L'eilah
(l'eilah) min kol birchata
v'shirata, tushb'chata
v'nechemata, da'amiran
b'alma, v'imru Amein.

יִתְבָּרַךְ וְיִשְׁתַּבַּח וְיִתְפָּאַר
וְיִתְרוֹמַם וְיִתְנַשֵּׂא, וְיִתְהַדָּר
וְיִתְעַלֶּה וְיִתְהַלַּל שְׁמֵהּ
דְּקֻדְשָׁא, בְּרִיךְ הוּא. לְעֵלָּא
(לְעֵלָּא) מִן כָּל־בִּרְכָתָא
וְשִׁירָתָא, תֻּשְׁבְּחָתָא וְנֶחֱמָתָא,
דַּאֲמִירָן בְּעָלְמָא, וְאִמְרוּ אָמֵן.

Y'hei sh'lama raba min
sh'maya, v'chayim aleinu
v'al kol Yisrael, v'imru
Amein.

יְהֵא שְׁלָמָא רַבָּא מִן שְׁמַיָּא,
וְחַיִּים עָלֵינוּ וְעַל כָּל־יִשְׂרָאֵל,
וְאִמְרוּ אָמֵן.

POPLARS

by Henryk Grynberg

They stand in a row like chimneys,
sooty Italian poplars
signposts to heaven
tall
like the local silence
they grew here all the time
in spite of
and above all
and they're still growing

while the air here is thick
with absence
clouds of absence in the air
and an emptiness called forgetting
ascends to heaven like a cloud

trodden by feet in the millions
the great Auschwitz field
the Auschwitz field of Maidanek
the Auschwitz field of Treblinka
the Auschwitz field of All This

on which we stand
move with us
wherever we try to go
so one can't get anyplace from here
nor leave here

I halted in the row of poplars
and try to grow along with them
and like them to gaze
upwards
with green eyes
I don't try to understand anything
nor say anything
what else can one
have to say here

I come here to add my own
to the growing silence

CHAPTER I

An Introduction to Polish Jewry Culture

On October 22, 1987, El Al Israel Airlines' Serial #4X-ABN flew nonstop from Warsaw to Tel Aviv, establishing the link between what was before World War II the largest Jewish community in Europe and Israel. LOT Polish Airlines flew Lockheed Electra in October 1938 from Warsaw with landings in Lvov, Bucharest, Sofia, Salonika, Athens, Rhodes and Nicosia before landing at Lydda (now Ben-Gurion Airport). This event followed the reestablishment of relations between Poland and Israel which were broken after the Six-Day War in 1967. Since then thousands of Israelis, many of them young, have visited Poland in search of their roots, as well as to learn the tragic history of the Shoah. They were following in the footsteps of American, Canadian and European Jews who made the pilgrimage to Kever Avot before them.

Of the more than 15 million Jews in the world today, half are emotionally linked with the heritage of the Polish Jewry. Before the war the Jewish community of Poland, the largest Jewish community in Europe and second largest in the world, comprised some 10 percent (while paying 35 percent of taxes) of the Polish population, which according to the 1931 census was 32 million. In towns, the percentage was even higher and reached 33 percent in Warsaw (more than the Jewry of France), 75 percent in Pinsk and 51 percent in Bialystok.

Ibrahim Ibn Jakob, a Jewish traveler from Spain, was the author of the first written document about Poland. In the account of his journey in the years 960-965 he writes, among others, about "Mieszko's Land." There is a legend that ascribes the first Jewish settlement in Poland to a heavenly command to wandering Jews to "Polin" (Rest here). Some consider it a pun and attribute it to Rabbi Moshe Isserless of Cracow (Remu).

The first Jewish settlers in Poland came in the seventh to ninth centuries; but more numerous waves of settlers arrived in Poland between the twelfth and fifteenth centuries when Crusades and wars brought in their wake persecution of Jews in the countries of Western Europe. Jews found protection and tolerance in Poland, a country in need of enterprising Jewish merchants and craftsmen. In Poland, the Jews obtained "privileges" from Kings Boleslaus the Pious in 1264 and Casimir the Great a hundred years later; legend has it that privileges were granted in some measure because of Casimir's love for a Jewish girl named Esther (Esterka). The legend also says that the sons of this liaison were brought up as Christians and the daughters as Jews.

There also were valid, practical reasons to welcome Jews after the Mongol invasion, which left vast territories depopulated. The Polish rulers sought immigrants from the West including Jews. The insecurity and fear resulting from the Crusades and massacres in German-Moravian-Bohemian towns made the Jews eager to move east. The Jews were engaged at the time in trade and crafts, banking and tax collecting; they took inns, mills and distilleries on lease and were active in other areas of economic life; sometimes in agriculture (the 1931 census shows 135,000 Jews employed in agriculture!). In international trade they provided important links with the Moslem world. The fourteenth century saw the establishment of Jewish communities in Lvov, Sandomierz, Poznan, Brzesc and Troki. At the end of the fifteenth century there were in Poland up to 30 thousand Jews. On Poland's unification, King Casimir the Great (Kazimierz Wielki) ratified and broadend the statute in 1334, 1364, and 1367. The protected occupation was of moneylending.

Jewish presence at the same time was marred by massacres during the Black Death and the official anti-Jewish policy initiated in Wroclaw (Breslau) in 1267 by the Church Council. The legal position of Jews in the sixteenth and seventeenth centuries was reaffirmed by various Polish leaders as well as underminded by some decrees of "Privilegia De Non-Tolerantis Judaeis."

In Lithuania, part of the Polish Union in which the Jews were originally welcomed, they were expelled in 1495 and readmitted in 1503. Various forms of Jewish autonomy existed, the most well known being the Council of Four Lands *(Va' ad Arbaa Aratzoth)*.

The Chmielnicki's Ukrainian revolt and subsequent wars with Moscow and Sweden decimated the Jewish community. However, by 1764 the census noted that it had grown to 750,000.

By the latter part of the eighteenth century, the Jewish community was spread among Russia, Austria and Germany following Poland's partition. The new situation deeply affected the Jewish community structures. Many enlightened Polish leaders like Kollataj and Chapski promoted Jewish emancipation while Staszyc and Czartoryski demanded an end of the "Jewish state within the state." Toward the end of the nineteenth century the Jews in economic terms constituted the urban middle class as well as the factory and workshop proletariat.

In time Poland became a powerful center of Jewish culture. The Jewish population included both the Ashkenazim and the Sephardim, who fled from Spain and Portugal in the fifteenth century. This cultural differentiation of the Jewish community in Poland bred a specific type of Polish Jew and in the eighteenth to nineteenth centuries led to clashes among various religious and cultural currents; between Hassidim and the progressive "Enlightenment," and cultural assimilation movements such as Maskilim. Most Jews held fast to their traditional religious and cultural customs and preserved their identity; others, in the minority, aspired to join Polish society, frequently at the cost of their religious faith.

The middle of the ninteenth century saw the Kronenberg, Natanson, Epstein, Wawelberg, Rotwant, Toeplitz, Reichman and Bloch families organize and develop many facets of Poland's economic and cultural life. They were pioneers of the country's modern banking system and industry, of engineering, paper trade and transport (e.g., railway lines linking Warsaw with Vienna, Terespol and Lodz, as well as navigation on the Vistula River). Polish Jews initiated the development of the phonographic and film industries. They generally contributed to the expansion of towns and the flowering of Polish urban culture; they had their share in the development of Polish book publishing (the Orgelbrands, Glucksbergs, Merzbachs, Lewentals, Ungers and Mortkowiczs) and the Polish press.

In addition to such renown writers as Isaak Peretz, Shalom Asch and Shalom Aleichem, who wrote in Yiddish, Jews also were active in Polish-language literature, arts and music. In the ninteenth century, for example, the directors of the Warsaw Opera House were, among others, Adam Munchheimer and Ludwik Grossman, a composer and piano manufacturer; while the co-founder and builder of the Warsaw Philharmonic Hall, opened in 1901, was Aleksander Reichman.

Jews took an active part in the Polish national liberation movement during the Kosciuszko insurrection in 1794, the November insurrection of 1830-1831, the January insurrection of 1863, the revolt of 1905, the struggles for independence in 1918, and also in the battles against Poland's occupiers in World War I. Some served with Pilsudski's legions. The majority, however, lived a separate life apart from Polish society, were Orthodox and spoke Yiddish. Many lived in a shtetl which according to Moshe Glaser's definition should have four essential elements:

1. *Mestechko* (small town in Polish [Miasteczko])
2. Three *minyans* to support a rabbi and a prayer house
3. A *cheder* (Jewish elementary school)
4. A *marchatz* (public bath).

Independent Poland, which was reborn after World War I, was a country of minorities such as Jews, Bialorussians, Ukrainians, and Germans. The Treaty of Versailles provided for protection of minorities. The Polish treaty even included provisions for Jewish schools and respect of Shabbath, but in practice it did not work out quite this way. Use of Yiddish and Hebrew was discouraged, and "numerus clausus" restricted Jewish education in Polish high schools and universities.

The economic situation of the Jews in the 1930s took a turn for the worse and many had to rely on foreign aid. This also led to the growth of the Zionist movement which included Hehalutz, Hehalutz Hatzair, Hashomer Hatzair, General Zionist and Labor Zionist groups.

During the "reign" of Marshall Pilsudski the situation of Jews in Poland was bearable in spite of economic and political pressure. It took the turn for the worse after his successors took over in the 1930's.

The outbreak of World War II brought devastation and eventually annihilation to the Jewish community of Poland. During the September campaign of 1939, 30 percent of all Jewish buildings were destroyed. Twenty thousand Jewish civilians lost their lives, as well as 32,216 officers and soldiers. Sixty-one thousand became POWs and very few survived. This Nazi persecution occurred in the first days of the conquest of Poland. Synagogue burnings, humiliations and arrests became everyday occurrences. By 1944 Poland became the largest Jewish cemetery in the world. The martyrdom and struggle of Polish Jewry will be described in different parts of this book.

The Jewish population of Poland developed numerous political parties including the left-wing Bund, Poalei Zion, the Communists, the Centrist Folkists, and the right-wing General Zionists, as well as Orthodox Jewish groups such as: "Mizrahi" and "Aguda." There also were Jewish groups aspiring to assimilation within the Polish community and strong Jewish trade unions. Jews had their representatives in both chambers of the Polish parliament as well as in many local town councils.

Jews were active in trade, crafts, industry, and also the

legal, medical and other professions. Some worked as agents of large and primarily absentee landowners, an occupation which in no small measure gave rise to anti-Semitism. They played an outstanding role in the development of towns and industry. In Lodz, for example, in spite of the influence of foreign capital, the textile industry was largely in the hands of prominent Polish Jewish families such as the Wislickis, Poznanskis, Kohns and Ettingers. The most active Jewish industrial and cultural centers were Warsaw, Cracow, Lodz, Lublin, Bialystok, Zamosc, Kalisz and until World War II Lvov (Lwow) and Wilna (Wilno, now Vilnius), both of which at that time were parts of Poland. Jews contributed significantly to the development of urban housing and to other residential facilities. They built their own public buildings, schools and theaters, synagogues, houses of prayer and cemeteries, hospitals and orphanages, as well as museums with unique collections, archives and libraries in larger towns. In the majority of Polish urban centers, the Nazis not only destroyed the Jewish community but also their monuments. However, some survived in Warsaw, Cracow and other towns.

The contribution of Polish Jewry covered many fields of human endeavor, but first and foremost was Judaic studies. Volumes would be necessary to deal with such a wide and rich subject, so only a few outstanding contributors can be mentioned here:

Judaic Studies

Moses Isserles (Remu) a the head of the Cracow Yeshiva and follower of Maimonides, wrote an adaptation of Shulchan Arukh to meet the needs of the Ashkenazi Jews.

Mordechai Jaffe, author of *Levushim*, Yehoshua Ben Alexander Hacohen Falk, rector of Lvov (Lwow) Yeshiva and commentator of Shulkhan Arukh.

Yom Tov Lippman Heller, commentator of the Mishnah.

Jacob of Belzec, author of *Dialogue with Marcin Czechowic.*

The Karaite Isaac Abraham Troki author of *Hizuk Emunah.*

Other famous rabbis were: Rabbi Solomon Luria, Abra-

ham Ben Shabbetai Horowitz, Jacob Ben Samuel
Bunim Koppelman, Mordechai Ben Abraham Jaffe and
Eliezer Mann.

Anshel of Cracow, who published the first book in Yiddish
in 1534 in order to spread knowledge of the Bible
among women who knew no Hebrew.

Rebecca, daughter of Rabbi Meir Tikitner (of Tykocin)
who published books of instructions as well as songs for
women.

Rabbi Joseph Pollack of Cracow, who established the prin-
ciple of "pilpul" (Pepper), a method in theological writings.

Yom Tov Lipman Muchausen of Cracow, who wrote *Sefer
Hanitzachon.*

The Haskalah movement, which was represented by: Is-
rael Ben Moses, Halevy Zamosc, Solomon Ben Yoel
Dubno, Solomon Maimon, Menahem Mendel Lewin of
Satanow, and Doctor Moses Marense.

The "Enlightened Talmudist" Rabbi Elijah Ben Solomon
Zalman (Gaon of Vilna).

Kabbalists: Isaiach Ben Abraham Halevi and Horowitz of
Kazimierz, author of *Shnei Luhot Habrith.*

The Hassidic movement, which was led by Israel Ben-
Eliezer (Ba'al Shem Tov) and Rabbi Jacob Joseph of
Polomoye. (The Hassidic movement emerged as a domi-
nant factor of the Polish Jewry in the eigteenth century. It opposed secular teaching and assimilation.)

Poland even had a false Messiah in Jacob Frank, the
leader of the Frankist movement, who upon arrival in
Poland from Bukovina announced himself as a successor of Shabetai Zevi and Messiah.

Leaders of the Zionist Movement

Menachem Begin
David Ben-Gurion
Itzhak Gruenbaum
Henryk Rosmaryn
Rabbi Osias
Itzhak Shamir
Emil Sommerstein
Rabbi Thon

Historians

Prof. Meir Balaban, Jewish history
Dr. Abramham Heschel, philosopher of religion
Prof. Mozes Schorr, Bible and Semitic languages
Prof. Edmund Stein, Hellenistic studies, midrash
Dr. Abraham Weiss, archaeology

Men of Letters

Abraham Joseph Sztybel Maecenas of Hebrew literature.
Bronislaw Natanson (1865 -1906), Maecenas of Polish literature, encouraged and published the works of world-famous writers Stefan Zeromski, Eliza Orzeszkowa, and Nobel Prize winner Wladyslaw Reymont.
Napoleon (Naphtali) Telz (1866-1943), publisher of newspapers
Dziennik Poranny, Dziennik Krakowski and Naprzod.
Samuel Orgelbrand, publisher of 1858 Universal Encyclopaedia.
Jakub Mortkowicz (1876-1931), co-founder of the Polish Book House, and "Ruch" Railways Bookshops, (seen all over Poland today).

Yiddish and Hebrew Writers

Shalom Jacob Abramovitsh   Uri Zvi Gniesin
  (Mendele Mocher Sefarim)   Itzhak Katzenelson
Shalom Aleichem   Jopseph Opatoshu
Sholem Asch   Isaac Leib Peretz
Micha Josef Berdyczewski   Issac Bashevis Singer
Isaiah Bershadsky   Hillel Zeitlin
Chaim Nachman Bialik

Polish Language Writers

Leopold Blumenthal   Jerzy Lutowski
Halina Gorska   Bruno Schulz
Janusz Korczak (Henryk Goldszmit) Bruno Winawer
Jerzy Kosinski   Stanislaw Wygodzki

Poets

Boleslaw Lesmian   Julian Tuwim
Itzik Manger (Yiddish)   Adam Wazyk

Anatol Slonimski   Josef Wittlin
Anatol Stern   Henryk Grynberg

Hebrew Translators of Polish Writers

Chaim Ben Abraham (Wladyslaw Reymont)
E.N. Frank and A. Lewinson (Henryk Sienkiewicz)
Judah Julian Klaczko and J. Lichtenbaym (Adam
   Mickiewicz)

Doctors Serving Polish Kings

John Albert (Casimir the Jagiellon)
Solomon Ashkenazi (Sigismund Augustus)
Menahem Simha Emmanuel de Yonah (John III Sobieski)
Joseph Solomon Delmedigo (1591-1655) a disciple of Gali-
   leo

Masters of the Theater

Esther Rachael Kaminska, "Mother of the Yiddish Theater" (mother of Ida and aunt of Danny Kaye).
Ida Kaminska (daughter of Esther), reestablished the
   theater after World War II.
Zygmunt Turkow (Ida's husband), managed the theater.

Cantors

Moshe Abram Bernsztajn
Eliezier Gerszowich
Moshe Kusewicki
Jakub Shmuel Morogowski
Josele Rosenblat (American who frequently visited Poland)
Pinchas Szerman

Choirs

In between World Wars I and II, there were a number of
choirs in many towns. The most famous was the Lodz
Choirs "Hazamir" Nightingale. Another one, consisting of
100 singers, was under the leadership of Dawid Ajzensz-
tadt (1890-1942) at the Tlomackie Synagogue of Warsaw.
Its concerts were even broadcast over Polish radio. Famous choir masters in that period included:

Dawid Bajgelman (1887-1944)

21

Abraham Cwi Dswidowica (1877-1942)
Izrael Fajwyszys (1887-1942)
Jakub Gladszrein (1885-1942)
Leo Liow (1878-1963)
Abraham Sliep (1884-1942)
Mosze Szneur (1885-1942)

Most of them perished in the Holocaust.

Folk Artists/Singers

Mordko (Mordechai) Fajerman, who was prototype of Jankiel in *Pan Tadeusz* (Polish national epic) by Adam Mickiewicz.

Mordecai Gebirtig, his "S'brent Undzer Shtetl Brent" (Our Town Is On Fire) became the hymn of the fighting ghettos.

Minters

Jews were minters to some Polish kings and dukes, and some early twelfth-century coins bear the names of Abraham, Yosef, Yaacov and Menahem, as well as the words *Beracha, Beracha Vehatzlaha, Beracha Tova*, etc. One bears the inscription *Beracha Casi* ("Blessing to Casimir"). These "Hebrew" coins were minted in Poland after a one thousand year interval since the last Hebrew coins previously had been minted by Bar Kochba.

Musicians

Adam Furmanski
Pawel and Eli Kochanski

Ludwik Urstein
Grzegosz Piatigorski

Some Artists of Polish-Jewish background became world famous and are too numerous to mention. The best example would be Arthur Rubinstein (after whom the philharmonic orchestra of his home town, Lodz, is named).

Composers

Zygmunt Bialostocki, his hits were sung by Bing Crosby and Doris Day.

Jerzy Petersburski, wrote the world renowned "Donna Clara" and "Amour Disait Folie" which became part of Edith Piaf's repertoire.

Painters

The collection of the Museum of the Jewish Art, attached to the Jewish Historical Institute, includes paintings by such famous artists as Maurycy Gottlieb, Maurycy Trebacz, Artur Markowicz, Jan Gotard, Adolf Behrman, Marcin Kitz, Bruno Schulz, Jonasz Stern, and Marek Wlodarski as well as sculptures and works in metal by Abraham Ostrzega, Jozef Gabowicz, Henryk Glicenszsten, Jozek Sliwiak, Henryk Kuna, Alina Szapocznikow, and Romuald Gruszczynski.

Some paintings dealing with Jewish themes can be seen at other museums including the following:

National Museum in Warsaw (Muzeum Narodowe), 3 Al. Jerozolimskie
The Anger of Saul with David by Antoni Brodowski
Jewish Feast (Swieto Trabek; Tashlich) by Aleksander Gierymski
Portrait of Young Girl by Mojzesz (Moise) Kisling
Umbrella and the Invisible by Tadeusz Kantor
Casimir the Great and Jews by Wojciech Gerson
Death of Berek Joselewicz at Kock by Henryk Pillati

National Museum (Muzeum Narodowe) in Cracow, Ul. 3 Maja: 1
The Maccabees by Wojciech Korneli Stattler
Ahasverus by Maurycy Gottlieb

National Museum in Poznan:
Ramamagauga by Tadeusz Cantor

Museum of Art in Lodz:
A Worthless Cargo by Jerzy Krawczyk

Lublin Palace:
Bringing Jews to Poland by Jan Matejko

In the summer of 1989 a massive exhibition entitled "The Jews of Poland" was organized by the National Gallery in Cracow. It included 1,400 paintings either by Jewish artists or dealing with the Jewish themes. The paintings came from museums and other educational institutions from many parts of Poland. Among them were:

The Art Museum in Lodz
The Czartoryski Collection in Cracow
The Jagiellonian University in Cracow
The Jewish Historical Institute in Warsaw
The National Gallery in Cracow
The National Gallery in Poznan
The National Gallery in Warsaw
The National Gallery in Wroclaw
The National Library in Warsaw

The exhibition included such giants of Polish art as:

Aleksander Gierymski
Maurycy Gottlieb and his brothers
Aleksander Lesser
Jacek Malczewski
Jan Matejko(the national painter of Poland.)

Those paintings by Aleksander Sochaczewski (1843-1923) depicting the Polish martyrdom in Siberia are on permanent exhibit at the Warsaw Citadel. A scaled-down version of the exhibition moved to Zacheta Gallery in Warsaw, and there are plans to bring it to the United States.

Jewish Press

This list would not be complete without the mention of

the Jewish Press. Between 1918 and 1939 (before World War II), 30 dailies and 130 Jewish periodicals were published in three languages. Among them are *Nasz Kurier, Nasz Przeglad, Maly Przeglad* (edited by Janusz Korczak), *Dziennik Warszawski, Nasz Glos Warszawy, Yiddish Telegrafen Agentur (JTA)*, founded by Mendel Mozes and in existence today in the U.S.A., and many others.

During the war in addition to the "official" *Gazeta Zydowska,* some 70 clandestine newspapers were published between 1940 and 1943. At the present time the Cultural and Social Union publishes *Yiddish Weekly Folks Sztym,* the only Yiddish weekly in the Eastern bloc.

To sum up what remains of such a rich heritage one can quote a poem of Antoni Slonimski:

> Gone now are those little towns where the shoemaker was a poet,
> The watchmaker a philosopher, the barber a troubadour.
> Gone now are those little towns where the wind joined
> Biblical songs with Polish tunes and Slavic rue,
> Where old Jews in orchards in the shade of cherry trees
> Lamented for the holy walls of Jerusalem.
> Gone now are those little towns, though the poetic mists,
> The moons, winds, ponds, and stars above them
> Have recorded in the blood of centuries the tragic tales,
> The histories of the two saddest nations on earth.

Polish Jewry Today

Today there is only a tiny Jewish community in Poland; probably well under 10,000 in total, including some modern-day "Marranos," of which about 5,000 maintain an active contact with Jewish institutions. All that is left of the world which is no more is its heritage, monuments and cemeteries.

Jewish life in Warsaw now centers around the Jewish Religious Organization (*Zwiazek Religijny Wyznania Mojzeszowego*), located next to the renovated Nozyk Synagogue on Twarda Street, and the Cultural Association (*Towarzystwo Kulturalne Zydow w Polse*), located on the Plac Grzybowski next to the Yiddish Theater (*Panstwowy Teatr Zydowski imienia Ester R. Kaminskiej*). The same building houses also *Folks-Sztym*, a Jewish newspaper published in Yiddish and Polish.

The Esther Rachel Kaminska State Jewish Theater also located there stages masterpieces of Jewish drama. This is the only state subsidized Jewish theater in the world. Many Poles and foreigners attend the theater, where earphones are provided to give simultaneous translations in Polish for the Polish audience. Unfortunately no other translations are offered.

Small communities or "active" synagogues still exist in Bielsko-Biala, Bytom, Czestochowa, Dzierzoniow, Gliwice, Katowice, Krakow, Legnica, Lodz, Lublin, Szczecin, Walbrzych, Wroclaw, and Zary.

An organization deserving a very special mention is JDC—the American Jewish Joint Distribution Committee or "Joint" has played an important role in the Jewish life of Poland. JDC returned to Poland in 1981, and today its programs reach about 4,500 Jews whose average age is 78. JDC provides cash relief for the needy and health services, such as medicines, hearing aids and eyeglasses that are not available locally,. Eight kosher kitchens provide 75 thousand free meals a year.

JDC programs also include weekly cultural activities in Jewish clubs: performances by the Yiddish Theater, Jewish films followed by lectures, evenings of Jewish music or lectures with slides.

JDC provides funds for the Jewish Religious Congregation, which makes religious suppiles such as matzot, lulavim and ethrogim available to the community.

Since 1987, JDC has supported a program for young people age 20 to 45. Generally the children of mixed marriage, they have begun to rediscover and explore their Jewish roots. They attend lectures in Jewish culture and tradition, study Hebrew and Yiddish, and attend summer camp and monthly winter retreats in Srodborow. By 1990, about 350 young people participated in this program.

Since 1987 an organization which became extremely important in supporting the remnants of the Polish Jewry is the Ronald S. Lauder Foundation. Its activities include maintenance of the cemeteries, providing religious leadership, supplying books for the younger generation and organizing activities such as concerts. It was also instrumental in establishing the first Jewish kindergarten. It also cooperates with experts from Poland and the United States in assessing the conservation needs of the Auschwitz camp site. Rabbi Chaskel Besser of the foundation is a frequent visitor to Poland.

According to the Polish Ministry of Religions survey made in 1974, only 22 out of 434 cemeteries were in relatively good condition. Seventy-eight were nearly totally destroyed and the rest were partially destroyed.

There are other "Jewish-oriented" organizations in existence in Poland. The International Janusz Korczak Society honors Dr. Janusz Korczak (Henryk Goldszmit) who perished in Treblinka with the children from his orphanage. Dr. Korczak was an internationally known educator and writer of children's books. The Poles consider him a Polish national hero as much as a Jewish one and hundreds of educational and youth institutions are named after him. The society cooperates closely with Kibbutz Lochamey Hagetaot.

Another institution is the Polish Association of Righteous Gentiles (second in size to that of Holland), which came into being only recently after years of keeping a very low profile. Close to three thousand Poles (approximately 34 percent of the total) were honored by Yad Vashem as of January 1990. After a painful amnesia of some 40 years on matters Jewish, there is an unusual interest in the subject, particularly among the Polish intelligentsia.

A number of books have been published on Judaism, Shoah and even Jewish cooking. Some are in English or German but unfortunately the bulk are in Polish, which makes them inaccessible to most people.

The famous Jagiellonian University of Cracow (and one of the oldest universities in Europe) established the Institute for Polish-Jewish Studies under the directorship of the former university's rector Prof. Jozef Gierowski, who is assisted by Joachim Russek, a historian.

The world-famous Polish movie producer Andrzej Wajda has staged *Dybuk* both in Jerusalem and in Cracow. His most recent accomplishment is a film on the life of Janusz Korczak.

The Israeli Philharmonic and other Israeli theatrical groups visit Poland. During one visit world-renowned violinist Itzhak Perlman and Israel Philharmonic members gave an impromptu recital at the Femina Cinema. It was at this formerly Jewish owned theater that the Jewish Symphony Orchestra performed for residents of the Warsaw ghetto from 1940 to 1942.

In the United States a foundation for the Polish-Jewish studies has been established under the leadership of the author Jerzy Kosinski.

Polin is a journal of Polish-Jewish studies published in Oxford as a result of international cooperation between scholars in England, Israel, Poland and the United States.

Malgorzata Niezabitowska, author of *Remnants: The Last Jews of Poland* (together with her husband Tomasz Tomaszewski), became a minister and spokesperson in the new Polish government in 1989.

The Polish-Israel Friendship League was created recently by some young leading members of the Jewish community. It is headed by Senator Andrzej Szczypiorski (author of *The Beautiful Mrs. Seidenman*). Other prominent members of the league are Professor Jozef Gierowski, Dr. Andrzej Friedman, Professor Jerzy Tomaszewski, and Jerzy Turowicz (editor-in-chief of Tygodnik Powszechny.) The League plans to move to its own premises at Cafe Eilat on Aleje Ujazdowskie near Plac Trzech Krzyzy.

As the complex and painful Polish-Jewish relations inched toward a better understanding, they suffered a serious setback over the Carmelite Convent of Auschwitz controversy.

The new democracy with its freedom for all gave also freedom of expression to the Rightist movement of the "Grunwald" type. Even the latest presidential elections gave expression to some anti-Semitic undertones. The future is frought with uncertainties, but for the disappearing Jewish community of Poland it seems somewhat academic.

P.S. As the book goes to print, President Lech Walesa

returned to Poland after a historic visit to Israel as a first Polish president, possibly marking a new chapter in the Polish Jewish relations.

PRESENT-DAY POLAND

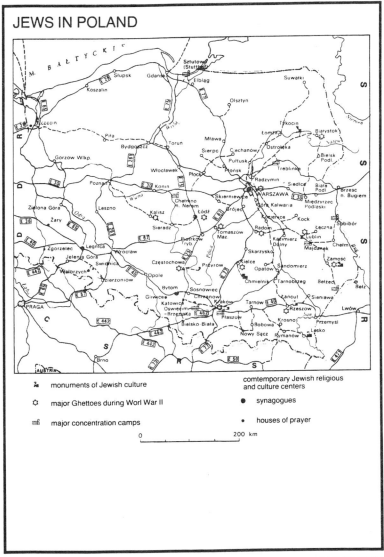

JEWS IN POLAND

𝕛 monuments of Jewish culture	comtemporary Jewish religious and culture centers
✡ major Ghettoes during Worl War II	● synagogues
⊨ major concentration camps	· houses of prayer

0   200 km

COURTESY OF ORBIS

THE GENERAL GOVERNMENT
OF POLAND, 1921-1939

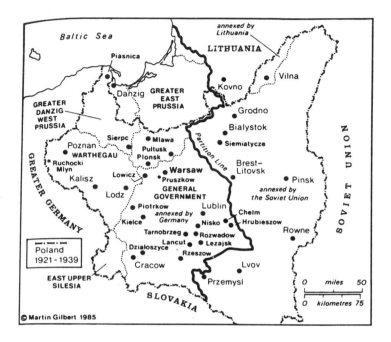

COURTESY OF MARTIN GILBERT

JEWISH COMMUNITY
ON THE EVE OF WORLD WAR II

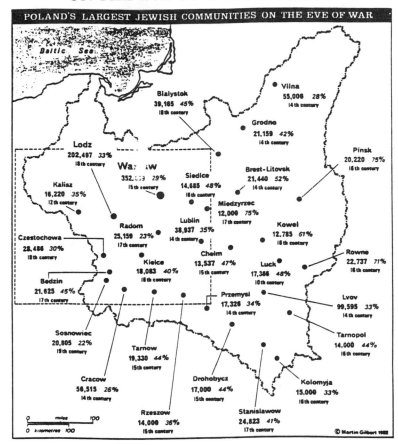

POLAND'S LARGEST JEWISH COMMUNITIES ON THE EVE OF WAR

Baltic Sea

Vilna
55,006 *28%*
14 th century

Bialystok
39,165 *45%*
18th century

Grodne
21,159 *42%*
14 th century

Lodz
202,497 *33%*
18th century

Pinsk
20,220 *75%*
16 th century

Warsaw
352,009 *29%*
15th century

Siedlce
14,685 *48%*
18 th century

Brest-Litovsk
21,440 *52%*
14 th century

Kalisz
16,220 *35%*
12 th century

Miedzyrzec
12,000 *75%*
17th century

Radom
25,159 *23%*
17th century

Lublin
38,937 *35%*
14 th century

Kowel
12,783 *67%*
16 th century

Czestochowa
28,486 *30%*
18th century

Chelm
13,537 *47%*
15 th century

Rowne
22,737 *71%*
16 th century

Kielce
18,083 *40%*
16 th century

Luck
17,366 *48%*
10 th century

Bedzin
21,625 *45%*
17th century

Przemysl
17,326 *34%*
14 th century

Lvov
99,595 *33%*
14 th century

Sosnowiec
20,805 *22%*
19th century

Tarnopol
14,000 *44%*
16 th century

Tarnow
19,330 *44%*
15th century

Cracow
56,515 *26%*
14 th century

Drohobycz
17,000 *44%*
15th century

Kolomyja
15,000 *33%*
16 th century

Stanislawow
24,823 *41%*
17th century

Rzeszow
14,000 *36%*
15 th century

miles 100

kilometres 100

© Martin Gilbert 1982

COURTESY OF MARTIN GILBERT

GERMAN-SOVIET PARTITION OF POLAND

COURTESY OF MARTIN GILBERT

THE JEWS OF POLAND, 1939-1945

THE JEWS OF POLAND 1939 - 1945

The Jews of Poland formed the largest single Jewish community in any of the States of inter-war Europe. In most Polish towns they constituted more than one-third of the total population. Amounting in all to 3,351,000 people by 1939, they provided one of the most flourishing cultural, political and social manifestations of Jewish life in the whole history of Jewish dispersal. Less than 369,000 survived the war, making a total death toll of at least 2,982,000 of whom nearly one million were teenagers, children under the age of 12, and babies.

SWEDEN

LITHUANIA

EAST PRUSSIA

GERMANY

MANY

CZECHOSLOVAKIA

Druja 1,000

Glubokoye 2,500

Vilna 45,000

Vileika 5,000

Molodechno 4,000

Lida 15,000

Nieswiesz 4,000

Novogrudok 2,500

Treblinka

Slonim 9,000

Kletsk 26 OCTOBER 1941 21 JULY 1942 4,000 1,000

Chelmno

Pinsk 28-31 OCTOBER 1941 30,000

Kovel 2 JUNE 1942 9,000

Sarny 3,000

Sobibor

Lutsk 20 AUGUST 1942 17,000

Belzec

Rovno 5 NOVEMBER 1941 15,000

Auschwitz

Dubno 27 MAY 1942 7,000

Kremenets AUGUST 1942 19,000

Tarnopol 5,000

Stanislav 12 OCTOBER 1942 10,000

RUMANIA

Regional deportations to death camps. Almost all those who were deported were murdered immediately on arrival.

Some of the towns whose entire Jewish populations were murdered following the German invasion of the Soviet Union on 26 June 1941. This map shows only a portion of such towns, with the approximate number of Jews killed, many of them in executions which lasted only *a single day,* and in circumstances of the most vile barbarity.

0 ____ 100 miles
0 ____ 100 km

— · — Poland's frontiers, 1920 - 1939.

—— The division of Poland between Nazi Germany and the Soviet Union, 28 September 1939 to 26 June 1941.

© Martin Gilbert 1978

COURTESY OF MARTIN GILBERT

JEWISH GHETTOS IN POLAND

JEWS FORCED INTO GHETTOS, OCTOBER 1939 TO DECEMBER 1940

COURTESY OF MARTIN GILBERT

NAZI CONCENTRATION CAMPS

THE CONCENTRATION CAMPS

Between 1939 and 1945, six million unarmed and innocent Jewish civilians - men, women, children and babies - were murdered in Nazi-controlled Europe, as part of a deliberate Nazi policy to destroy all traces of Jewish life and culture. As many as two million of these were killed in their own towns and villages, some confined in ghettoes where death by slow starvation was a deliberate Nazi policy, others taken to be shot at mass-murder sites near where they lived. The remaining four million Jews were forced from their homes and taken by train to distant concentration camps, where they were murdered by being worked to death, starved to death, beaten to death, shot, or gassed.

Among the hundreds of thousands of *non*-Jews sent by the Nazis to concentration camps were anti-Nazis, Jehovah's Witnesses, homosexuals, the mentally ill, and the chronically sick. In addition, more than 250,000 Gypsies were murdered, in a Nazi attempt to eliminate Gypsies as well as Jews from the map of Europe.

Auschwitz concentration camp in which more than 4 *million* people were murdered between 1941 and 1944, including Jews, Gypsies, and Soviet prisoners-of-war.

■ Camps set up solely for the murder of Jews.

卐 Other camps in which Jews and non-Jews were put to forced labour, starved, tortured, and murdered in conditions of the worst imaginable cruelty. Most of these camps had "satellite" labour camps nearby.

In many of the camps shown here so-called "medical" experiments were carried out, without anaesthetics, solely to satisfy the curiosity and sadism of the doctors. Hundreds of otherwise healthy "patients" were tortured and murdered during these experiments.

© Martin Gilbert 1978

0   100 miles
0   100 km

COURTESY OF MARTIN GILBERT

JEWISH MARTYRDOM AND RESISTANCE, 1939-1945

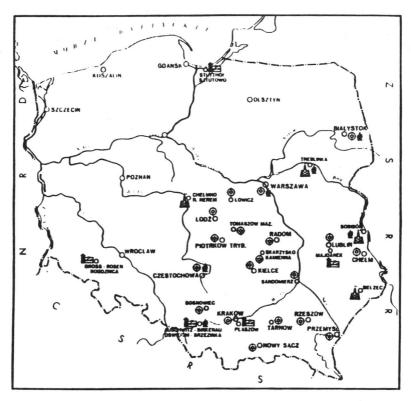

Concentration Camps

Centres of Immediate Extermination

Ghettos

Scenes of Uprisings and Armed Defence of the Jewish People

JEWISH REVOLTS, 1942-1945

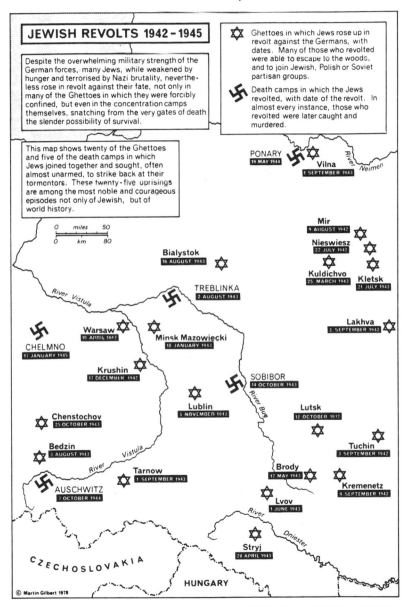

JEWISH REVOLTS 1942-1945

Despite the overwhelming military strength of the German forces, many Jews, while weakened by hunger and terrorised by Nazi brutality, nevertheless rose in revolt against their fate, not only in many of the Ghettoes in which they were forcibly confined, but even in the concentration camps themselves, snatching from the very gates of death the slender possibility of survival.

Ghettoes in which Jews rose up in revolt against the Germans, with dates. Many of those who revolted were able to escape to the woods, and to join Jewish, Polish or Soviet partisan groups.

Death camps in which the Jews revolted, with date of the revolt. In almost every instance, those who revolted were later caught and murdered.

This map shows twenty of the Ghettoes and five of the death camps in which Jews joined together and sought, often almost unarmed, to strike back at their tormentors. These twenty-five uprisings are among the most noble and courageous episodes not only of Jewish, but of world history.

O miles 50
O km 80

PONARY 19 MAY 1944

Vilna 1 SEPTEMBER 1943

River Neimen

Mir 9 AUGUST 1942

Niesviesz 22 JULY 1942

Kuldichvo 25 MARCH 1943

Kletsk 21 JULY 1943

Bialystok 16 AUGUST 1943

River Vistula

TREBLINKA 2 AUGUST 1943

Lakhva 3 SEPTEMBER 1942

Warsaw 19 APRIL 1943

Minsk Mazowiecki 10 JANUARY 1943

CHELMNO 17 JANUARY 1945

Krushin 17 DECEMBER 1942

SOBIBOR 14 OCTOBER 1943

River Bug

Lublin 3 NOVEMBER 1943

Lutsk 12 OCTOBER 1942

Chenstochov 25 OCTOBER 1943

Bedzin 3 AUGUST 1943

River Vistula

Tarnow 1 SEPTEMBER 1943

Brody 17 MAY 1943

Tuchin 3 SEPTEMBER 1942

Kremenetz 9 SEPTEMBER 1942

AUSCHWITZ 7 OCTOBER 1944

Lvov 1 JUNE 1943

River Dniester

Stryj 28 APRIL 1943

CZECHOSLOVAKIA

HUNGARY

© Martin Gilbert 1978

COURTESY OF MARTIN GILBERT

CHAPTER 2

Chronology of Jewish Presence in Poland

A.D.

860   Jewish merchant Ibn Kordabeh of Spain visits Poland.

960   Ibrahim Ibn Jakob, a Jewish traveler from Toledo,Spain, writes an extensive account about Poland entitled *Mieszko's Land*. (The first mention of Poland in history.)

1018   Due to persecution during the First Crusade, Jews migrate from Bohemia to Poland.

1096   First wave of Jewish migration to Poland escapes persecution during the first Crusade.

1147   Second wave of Jewish settlers arrive in Poland.

1264   Prince Boleslaw V the Pious of Kalisz issues the *Statute of Kalisz* writ, which establishes and protects Jewish legal position in Poland.

1267   Polish Church Council of Wroclaw (Breslau) outlines its anti-Jewish policies, seek-

	ing to segregate the Jews from the Christians.
1283	First Jewish cemetery is established in the town of Kalisz.
1334	King Casimir III the Great (Kazimierz Wielki) broadens and ratifies the *Statute of Kalisz*.
1399	First court case dealing with "ritual murder" marks the beginning of Jewish persecution.
1453	King Casimir IV Jagiello codifies the legal status of Jews. He entrusts salt mines and customs stations to Jewish managers.
1483	Expulsion of Jews from Warsaw.
1495-1503	Expulsion of Jews from Lithuania (then part of the Polish Union).
1495	Resettlement of Jews of Cracow in Kazimierz.
1507	King Sigisemund I the Elder reconfirms Jewish privilege.
1527	Warsaw introduces *privilegia de non tolerandis Judaeis* under Sigisemund I the Elder.
1534	King Sigisemund I the Elder decrees that Jews need not wear any distinguishing mark on their clothing. First Hebrew printing press established in Cracow.
1572	Death of Moshe Ben Israel Iserless (Remu).
1576	King Steven Batory decrees against accusations for ritual murder.
1579	Jewish Sejm (Parliament) convened.
1581-1764	Period of Jewish autonomy Sejm (Parliament of Four Lands [Va'ad Arbaa Aratzot]).
1648-1649	Chmielnicki, the Ukrainian Cossack nationalist revolt and massacres, Tatar incursions from Crimea and the Swedish War ravage Jews of eastern Poland.

39

1712	Jews expelled from Sandomierz.
1755	Jacob Frank starts Frankist movement.
1760	Death of Baal Shem Tov (Chassidic movement).
1764	Census in Poland-Lithuania counts 749,968 Jews.
1771	Eliahu Gaon of Vilna (Wilno) passes first curse on Chassidim.
1772	Enlightened Polish leaders, e.g., H. Kollataj and T. Czacki try to improve legal and social status of Polish Jews.
1791	Death of Jacob Frank. Constitution of May 3.
1794	Colonel Berek Joselewicz leads Jewish Legion in Kosciuszko's uprising against the Russians.
1797	Death of Eliahu Gaon of Vilna (Wilno), head of the Mitnagdim movement against Chassidim.
1807	Constitution of Duchy of Warsaw grants Jews equality.
1815	1,657 Polish Jews participate in Leipzig Fair.
1862	Despite emergence of wealthy Jewish merchant and financial class, the majority of Jewish merchants in Warsaw belong to the petty bourgeoise of shopkeepers.
1891	Imperial Russia's anti-Semitic May Laws are introduced into Poland.
1897	The anti-Semitic National Democratic Party (Endecja) is founded.
1897	Bund is founded.
1908	School quotas (*numerus clausus*) are imposed, resulting in the expulsion of many Jews from educational establishments.
1916	Agudat Israel is founded.
1921	Polish constitution of March 17 grants Jews equality and freedom of religion.
1922	General Zionist Party emerges as the domi-

	nant political force and voice of Polish Jewry.
1925	YIVO, the Institute for Jewish Studies (now located in New York City) is founded in Vilna (Wilno).
1930	Yeshivat Hachamei Lublin is founded.
1939	Jewish population of Poland numbers 3,351,000. Polish Jews suffer tremendous losses during the German invasion. In Warsaw alone, 30 percent of Jewish buildings are destroyed and 31,216 Jewish soldiers are killed. Privates Dawid Wachmeister and Lejb Katz were awarded order "Virtuti Militari" (the Polish equivalent of the Congressional Medal of Honor). Jewish Star introduced. First ghetto established in Piotrkow Trybunalski. (October 28, 1939)
1940	Ghettos established at: Czestochowa (March) Deblin (April), Jendrzejew (January), Plonsk (August), Tomaszow (June 1), Siedlce (May 6,), Warsaw (November 15,) Wroclawek (November), Zdunska (September), Lodz (December 1939), Lublin (beginning in 1940), and Cracow (March 1941).
1941	First inmates arrive at Auschwitz (Buna Camp) (I.G. Farben Company). Extermination camp is built at Chelmno on the Ner River.
1942	Wannsee Conference (January 20) sets the stage for the Holocaust. Death camps in Auschwitz (Oswiecim) Majdanek, Treblinka. Sobibor and Chelmo are established. First liquidation of the Warsaw Ghetto. First transport of Jews from Western Europe (France) arrives at Auschwitz followed by the Jews of Holland. Jewish Fighting Or-

ganization (*ZOB* [*Zydowska Organizacja Bojowa*]) is established. Council for the Assistance of the Jews (ZEGOTA) is established by Zofia Kossak and Wanda Filipowicz.

1943   Heroic revolt of Warsaw Ghetto (April 19,1943). Insurrection at the concentration camps of Treblinka (August 2) and Sobibior (October 14), led by Alexander Pechersky. Jewish partisans fight with the underground People's Guard (*Gwardia Ludowa*). Uprisings in the ghettos of Bialystok (August 16) Lublin (November 3), Czestochowa (October 25), Bedzin (August 3), Tarnow (September 1), Minsk Mazowiecki (January 10). Cracow Ghetto liquidated. Deportation of Jews from Greece and some countries of Western Europe.

1944   The Lodz Ghetto (the only one left in Europe) is liquidated and its population is deported to Auschwitz. Insurrection at Auschwitz (October 7). The Central Committee of Jews in Poland is established to assist Jewish survivors of the Holocaust.

1945   Revolt at Chelmno (January 17). 2,982,000 Polish Jews were killed during World War II. Only 55,509 survive. Total Jewish population reaches 250,000 after 154,000 are repatriated from the USSR.

1946   Pogroms in Cracow and Kielce.

1947   Jewish Historical Institute (*Zydowski Instytut Historyczny*) established.

1948   Poland recognizes Israel. A diplomatic legation is established.

1949   Jewish Religious Organization is established in Poland.

1950	End of mass emigration which depletes Polish Jewry.
1955	Jewish (Yiddish) State Theater is founded under Ida Kaminska.
1956	American Jewish Distribution Committee (Joint) renews operations in Poland.
1958	Fifty thousand Polish Jews emigrate from Poland.
1963	Israeli Mission to Poland is elevated to the level of embassy.
1968	Following a wave of government sponsored anti-Semitism, a fourth mass emigration of Polish Jews takes place.
1981	American Jewish Distribution Committee (Joint) reestablishes its operation in Poland.
1986	Israel Interest Section under Ambassador Mordechai Palzur established in Warsaw.
1987	El Al Airlines inaugurates Warsaw-Tel Aviv service by flying non-stop in $3^1/_2$ hours.
1990	Full diplomatic relations with Israel are reestablished at ambassadorial level (February 27).

CHAPTER 3

Glossary of Polish Jewry

ALEKSANDROW LODZKI (Aleksander)

Jewish cemetery (established in 1822) at Ulica Gorna. Only a few graves survived. One of those is that of Tzadik Dancygier.

AUGUSTOW

There were four thousand Jews residing here on the eve of World War II, mainly trading in timber. The ghetto was established in October 1941 and it was liquidated in August 1942 by deportation to Treblinka and Auschwitz. A cemetery devastated features a memorial stone for the victims of Shoah.

AUSCHWITZ-BIRKENAU (OSWIECIM-BRZEZINKA)

The concentration camp and death and work camp at Oswiecim, known as *Konzentrationslager Auschwitz (KL Au)*, was established on Himmler's orders on April 27, 1940. It was a complex of 40 camps, the biggest Nazi death factory *(Vernichtungslager)*, where up to 60 thousand people were murdered every day, mostly using Zyklon B gas. It has been preserved as a museum by the Polish government. In this 25-square-mile area, just over a one-hour drive from Cracow, the Nazis killed four million people, of whom three million were Jews.

AUSCHWITZ OVERVIEW

KRAKÓW

MYSLOWICE

OSWIECIM

BIELSKO

A. Mass Grave
B. Blocks
C. S.S. Mess
D. S.S. Camp
E. Railway Bridge
F. Monument
G. Castle and Tower
H. Tourist Center

45

PLAN OF AUSCHWITZ COMPLEX

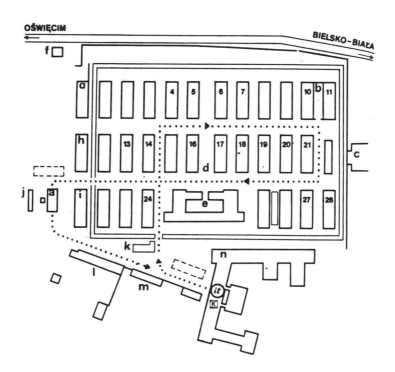

GENERAL EXHIBITION	NATIONAL EXHIBITIONS	PLACES OF SPECIAL INTEREST
4 - Extermination	13 - Denmark, Germany	a - Gas chamber & crematorium
5 - Material evidence of crimes	14 - U.S.S.R.	b - Wall of Death
6 - Everyday life of prisoners	15 - Poland	c - Store
7 - Living and sanitary conditions	16 - Czechoslovakia	d - Assembly Square
11 - Death Block	17 - Yugoslavia, Austria	e - Camp kitchen
	18 - Hungary, Bulgaria	f - Commandant's House
	20 - France, Belgium	g - Commandant's office and Gestapo
	21 - Italy, Netherlands	h - SS Administration
	27 - Suffering and stuggle of Jews	i - SS Hospital
		j - Political section (Camp Gestapo)
		k - Guardhouse
		l - SS garages
		m - Stores, warehouses, workshops
		n - Reception building for new prisoners
		Block 10 - Sterilization experiments
		Block 19, 20, 21, 23 - Prisoners hospital
		Block 24 - Museum Archive

The most recent study by the noted Holocaust scholar Yehuda Bauer shows that the total number of murdered victims at Auschwitz was about 1,350,000. Out of this number 1,323,000 were Jews. The four million figure, which notes only three-quarters as Jewish victims, was according to Professor Bauer an attempt to show that the Holocaust was not exclusively Jewish tragedy. At the present time the plaques, that are part of the Monument at Birkenau, are being changed to show the more historically accurate figure.

The trains arrived at Birkenau (Brzezinka), a few miles from Oswiecim. At the spot where the railway ramp ended and "selection" took place, there is a monument commemorating the four million people who perished there from 1940 to 1945. The commemoration stones are inscribed in Yiddish, Hebrew,and Polish, among the 18 languages. The monument was under restoration as of March 1990. Remnants of the crematoria blown up by the Nazis can be seen in the area of the monument. On both sides of the tracks stand remains of the wooden barracks that housed the prisoners.

On the Auschwitz side, a Jewish martyrdom pavilion (Cell Block #27) memorializes Hitler's six million Jewish victims. At the door a guest book signed by thousands of visitors to the pavilion is displayed. At the exit a slab is inscribed: "And the Lord said unto Cain, where is Abel thy brother? And He said, what has thou done? The voice of thy brother crieth unto Me from the ground." This pavilion is one of a number of "national" pavilions, which in a way perpetuate the myth that the Jews were just one of many nationalities murdered at Auschwitz. Other pavilions serve as a musesum of the death factory.

A Chronology of the Auschwitz Death Factory

1940

Apr. 27   Heinrich Himmler, Commander-in-Chief of
the SS, orders the construction of a
concentration camp on the site of the
former Polish artillery barracks at
Auschwitz. Factors that led to this de-

cision were the potential to physically expand the camp, its relative isolation, and the good railway connections to many parts of Europe.

May 4 Rudolf Hoess is officially appointed commander of Auschwitz.

May 20 The first inmates registered at Auschwitz are 30 convicted German criminals who were to serve as Kapos (inmate supervisors who enforced camp policy).

June 14 First transport of 728 Polish political prisoners arrive from Tarnow Prison.

1941

Mar. 1 More than ten thousand inmates are interned at Auschwitz. Heinrich Himmler visits Auschwitz, accompanied by officials of the I.G. Farben company, a major German industrial firm. Himmler orders the camp to be expanded to hold 30 thousand inmates and also the establishment of auxillary camps including a camp for the I.G. Farben Company with a capacity of ten thousand prisoners. This camp is known as the Buna Camp.

Summer Himmler orders Rudolf Hoess to make Auschwitz the center for the "Final Solution of the Jewish Question" (the Nazi code word for the total systematic murder of the Jews), according to Hoess' postwar testimony. By 1942, the majority of all new arrivals at Auschwitz are Jewish. Between 1942 and 1944, Jews are deported to Auschwitz from throughout occupied Europe.

Sept. 3 First experiments with the poison gas Zyklon B are conducted to find a method for killing large numbers of people quickly. The first victims are the sick inmates and Russian POWs.

Oct. 14　　Construction of a branch camp begins at Birkenau. It was originally intended for Russian POWs, ten thousand of whom already were interned at Auschwitz.

1942

Jan.　　Beginning of mass murder of Jews by poison gas at Birkenau.

Mar. 30　　First women inmates arrive at women's camp including 999 German women from Ravensbruck and 999 Jewish women from Slovakia.

Mar. 26-27　First transport of Jews from Western Europe (France) arrives at Auschwitz.

July　　Himmler's second visit to Auschwitz includes inspection of Birkenau where he witnesses the killing of inmates with Zyklon B poison gas in two cottages that were converted to serve as improvised gas chambers. Orders are issued to the Topf Company to construct four large crematoria with adjoining gas chambers. The previous installations were considered insufficient for the number of victims envisioned. The new installations were tested and put into operation between March-June 1943. The capacity for the two larger gas chambers was two thousand persons each.

July 17　　First transport of Dutch Jews arrives in Auschwitz.

Aug. 5　　First transport of Belgian Jews arrives in Auschwitz.

1943

Feb. 26　　Gypsy camp established at Birkenau. During 1942 to 1943, 40 satellite camps were created, and 28 of these camps

PLAN OF BIRKENAU (during the War)

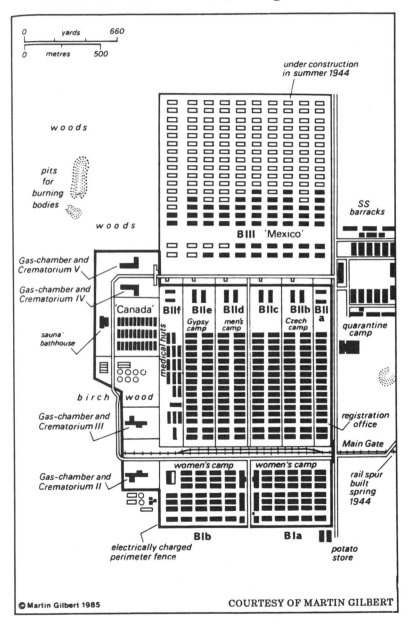

supplied slave labor to adjacent industrial plants. The main administration center for these camps was located at Auschwitz.

Mar. 15   Deportation of Greek Jews from Salonika to Auschwitz begins.

Oct.   After the partial German occupation of Italy, about 8,500 Jews were captured and sent to Auschwitz. By the end of 1943, Jews were the majority of inmates at Auschwitz- Birkenau.

1944

July-Aug.   425,000 Hungarian Jews sent to Auschwitz; 85 percent killed upon arrival.

Aug.   As a result of the advances of the Red Army on the Eastern Front, orders are given to phase out the activities at Auschwitz and eliminate all traces of the mass murder operations.

Oct. 7   Crematorium No. 3 is blown up forcing the revolt of the Sonderkommando (the Jewish inmates who were forced to remove the bodies from the gas chambers). Initially, the revolt was planned to include blowing up all the crematoria. Timing factors prevented the actualization of these plans.

Nov. 25   Nazis destroy the remaining crematoria and gas chambers.

1945

Jan. 18   Evacuation of Auschwitz and the beginning of the infamous Death Marches for those able to walk. Thousands die in these often aimless and cruel marches west toward Germany. Sick and disabled inmates are left behind.

Jan. 27   Russian troops, under Jewish Colonel Grigori Elishawetzki, liberate Auschwitz and the approximately 7,650 prisoners who remain.

Auschwitz (Oswiecim)

For a description of town of Oswiecim see p.102.

Baranow Sandomierski (Bornov)

The Jewish cemetery includes a mass grave of 60 Jews shot by the Germans.

Belzec

Belzec was a death camp established by the Germans in November of 1941 (and first reported to the West by Jan Karski). Six hundred thousand, mainly Jews from Poland, Czechoslovakia, Romania, Hungary, and Germany perished here. Upon liquidation of the camp in 1943, the Germans planted a forest to cover traces of their crimes. A memorial was built in 1963. The sculptor was Roman Dylewski; the designer was Mieczyslaw Welter.

PLAN OF THE CONCENTRATION CAMP AT BELZEC

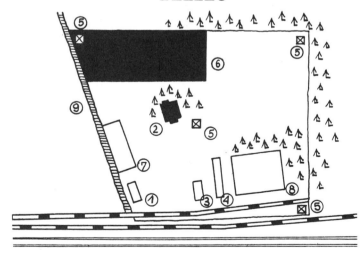

1. Guardhouse	5. Watch tower
2. Gas chambers	6. Mass graves
3. Place where prisoners undressed and left their clothes	7. Barracks
	8. Kitchens
4. Barrack	9. Anti-tank ditch

MAP SHOWING AREA NEAR BELZEC

COURTESY MARTIN GILBERT

Bedzin (Bendin)

The first Jews reached Bedzin in the seventeenth century and in the 20s were 60 percent of the population. They were active in industry and commerce. Germans destroyed the synagogue in the first days of September 1939. In May 1942 the first massive deportation to Auschwitz took place. The ghetto was established in January 1943 and liquidation in August 1943.

During the last deportation an armed resistance took place led by Frumka Plotnica who was killed in action.

A tablet at the courthouse at 22 Lipca 23 commemorates 200 victims of the Wermacht who were burned in the synagogue on September 9, 1939.

Biala Podlaska

A memorial located at the Jewish cemetery at Ulica (Street) Nowa commemorates 12 thousand Jews from Biala Podlaska, Augustow and Suwalek.

Bialystok

The Jewish Cemetery on Zabia (Street) is part of a public park, dominated by two large monuments, one commemorating the ghetto's dead, and the second one honoring Jewish partisans. The cemetery at Polnocna was established in 1890 and contains approximatley six thousand graves.

The Pogrom Memorial, a tall marble shaft in the old Jewish cemetery,commemorates the victims of the 1905 pogrom. The monument is inscribed with a poem by Zalman Shneour, a known Hebrew poet. The synagogue at Piekna 3, which was rebuit after the war, is now a youth house.

The Zamenhof Monument honors Dr. Ludwik Zamenhof, creator of the international Esperanto language, who was born in Bialystok in 1859.

A plaque at the Press House (*Dom Prasy*) at Ulica Wesolowskiego 1, a former synagogue, commemorates in Polish and Yiddish the three thousand Jewish victims burned alive on May 24, 1941. The plaque was affixed on the fifteenth anniversary of the Bialystok Ghetto Uprising (August 16, 1943).

A memorial contains ashes of 3,500 Jews killed during the Bialystok Ghetto Uprising, led by Mordechai Tenenbaum and Daniel Moszkowicz.

The Jewish school at Marchlewskiego 1, built about 1905, is today used as part of the Warsaw university.

A memorial tablet at Malmeda 10 honors Jewish resistance fighter Itzhak Malmed, who was killed by Germans on this spot.

Biecz (Beitch)

A monument honoring victims of the Holocaust at the Jewish cemetery at Ulica (Street) Tysiaclecia was errected at the mass grave. The synagogue is now a hotel.

Biedrzyce-Kozieglowy (Sypniewo Parish)

A tablet in the school courtyard marks the location of the work camp that existed from 1941 to 1942.

Bielsk Podlaski

The Jewish community goes back to the fifteenth century. The first synagogue was built in 1542. There were six thousand Jews in Bielsk in September 1939. This number included many refugees from the west who escaped to what was then Soviet-occupied Poland.

The ghetto was established at the end of 1941 and liquidated in 1942 by deportation to Treblinka.

The cemetery at Ulica Branska still has about one hundred matzcvot.

Bielsko Biala (Bielitz-Biala)

Congregation and house of worship is at Mickiewicza 26. Ahron Halbershtam, born in 1865, was appointed rabbi of Bielsko. The cemetery at Cieszynska 92 was established in 1849 with four hundred graves. The ghetto established in 1941 was liquidated in June 1940.

Bielzyce (Belshitza)

A monument remembers the 1,000 Jews of Bielzyce shot by the Germans on liquidation of the ghetto on May 8, 1943.

A cemetery and a monument (by the designer of "Memory Lane" in Warsaw) was erected in October 1990 by Nimrod Ariav (native of Israel) in honor of his father Arie Cygielman who was shot by the Germans on the square before the synagogue in October 1942.

Biernatki (Zelazkow County)

An obelisk commemorates 125 Jews shot in the forest on October 10, 1941. Their remains now rest at the Jewish cemetery of Kalisz.

Bilgoraj

The birthplace of Isaac Bashevis Singer.

The cemetery at Konopnickiej was restored through the

efforts of the Lumerman family. The cemetery at Morowa was completely destroyed. The memorial honors Jewish, Polish and Russian partisans executed in the woods of Rapy.

Bobowo

The ninteenth-century synagogue is now a school.

Bochnia

Jews came to Bochnia in the fifteenth century; and before World War II the population reached thirty-five hundred. About two thousand perished in Belzec; the remaning were killed in Auschwitz.

The cemetery, which was established in 1872, contain one hundred matzevot. There is a monument honoring the victims of the Holocaust. A memorial for victims of mass executions exists also at the communal cemetery, located at Orackiej.

The synagogue at Swierczewskiego now serves as offices. The synagogue at Warynskiego is now a restaurant called Sutoris.

Bodzentyn

The Jews came to Bodzentyn in the nineteenth century. The ghetto was liquidated by deportation of its inhabitants to Treblinka in November 1942. The famous diary of Dawidek Rubinowicz (the Polish equivalent of Anne Frank's diary) was found in Bodzentyn.

The cemetery at Gora Miejska established in 1867 still has some fifty-five matzevot.

Borownica

At the Jewish cemetery a stone marks the place where 100 Jews from the Radymno work camp were executed (October 1942).

Brzesko (Brigel)

The cemetery established in 1846, is well fenced and features one hundred matzevot. It was cleaned and renovated thanks to the initiative of Abe Hirsh from the United States. There is an obelisk on the grounds marking the mass graves of some five hundred Jews executed by the Germans.

The synagogue at Ulica Puszkina is now a municipal library.

Bydgoszcz

Jews came to Bydgoszcz in the eleventh and twelfth centuries. A synagogue was built in 1835. By 1939 there were some twenty-five thousand Jewish inhabitants. The main gate to Zachem chemical works comemorates British, Dutch and Belgian POWs, as well as Jews from Stutthof concentration camp.

Cmentarz Bohaterow (Heroes' Cemetery) at Ulica (Street) Przyjemna 1 Wzgorze Wolnosci has a plaque commemorating 2,500 Jewish inhabitants of Bydgoszcz.

The synagogue in Fordon is now a cinema.

Bytom

Jewish presence in Bytom dates back to 1349. By 1939, fourteen hundred Jews lived there. The congregation is at Smolenska 4; house of worship at Plac Grunwaldzki 62. A cemetery, which consists of about one thousand graves, is at Piekarska 56.

Cecylowka

A monument honors 54 victims of the Wehrmacht, who on September 13, 1939, were locked up in a barn and burned.

Chelmno (Cumhof on the Ner River)

Chelmno was established on December 8, 1941, and functioned until January 1945 as Sonderkommando Cumhof.

Monument to Nazi victims on the site of the Chelmno death (Cumhof) camp marks the first murder camp set up in occupied Poland by the Nazis, and memorializes 340 thousand Polish Jews and 20 thousand from other countries. Other victims were Russian POWs and 88 Czech children from Lidice. Another monument in front of the main Catholic church honors the Jews who staged an unsuccessful revolt against the Nazis.

PLAN OF CONCENTRATION CAMP AT CHELMNO

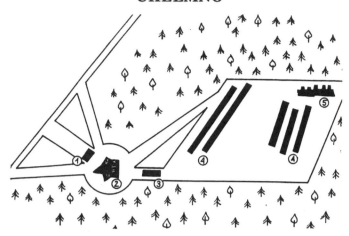

1. Grave of shot hostages
2. Monument-mausoleum
3. Children's quarters
4. Mass graves
5. Crematorium furnaces

CHELMNO MONUMENT

CHELMNO AREA

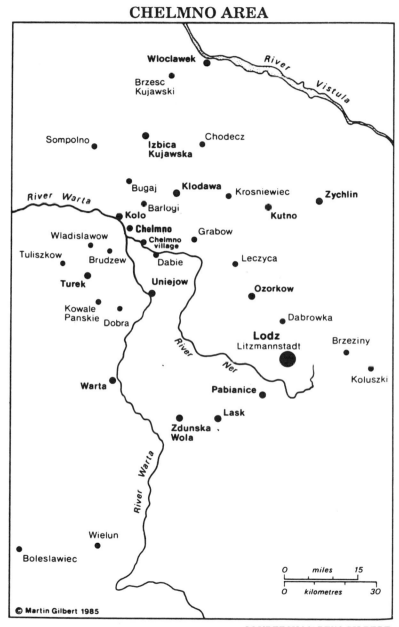

COURTESY MARTIN GILBERT

Checiny

The synagogue is now a cinema. The cemetery at Gora Zamkowa contains one hundred fifty graves, the oldest dating back to 1638.

Chelm

Jewish presence in Chelm goes back to 1442. The famous citizens of Chelm included Rabbi Yehuda Aron and Eliahu Baal Shem. Chelm was an important center of Polish Jewry and there were two Jewish weeklies before the war. On the eve of World War II there were fifteen thousand Jews in Chelm. The mass deportation took place in 1942.

The synagogue is now a technical school. The cemetery is at Starosinska.

Chmielnik

According to the 1921 census about fifty-nine hundred Jews lived in Chmielnik. The ghetto was established in April 1941 and liquidation took place in 1943 by mass deportation to Treblinka.

A synagogue of great architectural value was built in 1630-1634.

Chrzanow

There were about eight thousand Jews in Chrzanow before World War II. The ghetto, which was established in 1940, was liquidated in 1943. Most of the population perished in Auschwitz.

The synagogue is now a warehouse. Judaica is featured at Chrzanow Museum. The cemetery at Podwale has some 50 matzevot. The cemetery at Borowcowa contains about one thousand graves.

Ciechanow

The Jewish community of Ciechanow goes back to the sixteenth century. The ghetto was liquidated by deportation to the Mlawa ghetto and from there to Auschwitz.

A plaque at the parish house at Ulica (Street) Fabryczna commemorates the inmates of the penal camp. A devastated cemetery is at Pultuska.

Cieszanow

The synagogue at Skorupki 7 which was established in 1889, is now a warehouse. The cemetery was completely destroyed.

Cieszyn

A nearly destroyed synagogue is at Ulica Hazlaska 2. Cemeteries on the same street from the eighteenth and ninteenth centuries have some five hundred matzevot. There is also a monument at the cemetery on the spot of mass execution in 1944.

Tablet on the school wall is in memory of Jewish women at a nearby camp organized in 1944.

Czechowice-Dziedzice

A monument honors Jews from this branch of the Auschwitz camp shot by the Germans on the eve of liberation on January 19, 1945. Cemetery at Szolna has 50 matzevot.

Czestochowa (Chenstchov)

Jewish community in Czestochowa goes back to seventeenth century. The first Jewish settlers were employed in textile and tapestry industries.

By 1765, there were 51 Jewish families in Czestochowa. A Jewish cemetery was established in 1799; until that time burials took place at Janowo. A synagogue was also built at that time.

A more elaborate synagogue was built in 1899 at Spadek and Aleksandryjska Streets in a place occupied today by the Czestochowa Philharmonic.

On the eve of World War II, the Jewish population was forty thousand. Ulica Berka Joselewicza was named after Jewish colonel in the Kosciuszko national uprising.

A few famous Jewish citizens of Czestochowa to be mentioned are: Henryk Merkusfeld, a philantropist; Jan Glickson, a lawyer; and Edward Kohn, a doctor. Czestochowa was famous for the printing press of Samuel Kohn, Wilhelm Kohn, and Oderfeld brothers, which existed until the German occupation in 1940 and 1941 respectively. A number of

Jewish newspapers functioned in Czestochowa, one of them the Hajn lasted until World War II.

Czestochowa even had a Jewish theater which was funded by the Wohlberg family. It was situated at Aleje NMP 12.

Thirty thousand Czestochowa Jews perished in World War II, mainly in Treblinka, and today there are hardly any traces of that community.

A plaque (written in Polish and Hebrew) at Ulica (Street) Kawia 20 to 21, commemorates Jews shot during liquidation of the ghetto on September 24, 1942.

Mass grave and monument at the Jewish cemetery at the end of Ulica (Street) Zlota (Zawodzie District) commemorates the Jewish victims of Czestochowa, as well as members of the Jewish Fighting Organization (Z.O.B.).

During January 1943, an armed resistance took place under the leadership of Mendel Fiszelewicz. Miraculously 5200 Jews working in Hasag plant were saved when the red army entered the area.

Cracow (Krakow)

On the eve of World War II, 56 thousand of the 300 thousand inhabitants of Cracow were Jews. Today there are 700 thousand people in Cracow. The community goes back to the eleventh century, but it reached the peak of its development in the sixteenth century.

With transfer of Poland's capital to Warsaw, Cracow declined somewhat. However before 1939 it had a Hebrew high school, commercial school (with two thouand students), Mizrahi school, Yeshiva (sponsored by Agudat Israel), Jewish theater, Jewish hospital, library, its own newspapers *Woche* and *Nowy Dziennik* and other institutions.

Some important Jewish citizens of Cracow were Lewko, who administered the Royal Mint for Casmir the Great and was also a banker to King Wladyslaw Jagiello and Hungary's Ludovic; merchants Pinkas Horowic, Izaak Jakubowicz; Herbrew printers Asher, Eliakim and Samuel—sons of Chaim of Halicz, and Menachem Meisels and Izaak Prostitz. Another Jewish protege of a Polish king was Michal Ezofowicz, who was knighted by King Sigismund I in 1525.

Jews were active in Political life in Cracow in Bund, B'nai Brith, Poalei Zion, Mizrahi, as well as Polish socialist party. Zionist organizations such as Beitar, Menora, Brith Hayal and Vered were active in Cracow.

A Jewish theater functioned at 7 Bochenska Street.

During World War II Cracow was a seat of the German government in Poland and Hans Frank, the governor general established his residence at the Wawel Castle.

MAP OF KAZIMIERZ SYNAGOGUES

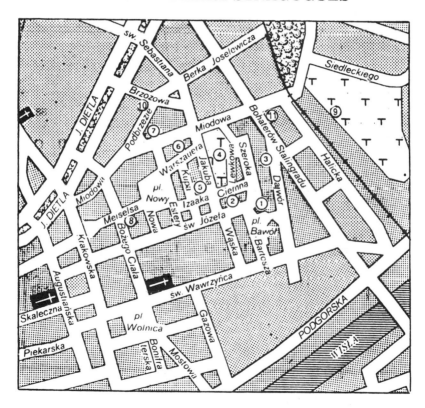

1. Old Synagogue (*Stara Boznica*)
2. High Synagogue (*Boznica Wysoka*)
3. Poper Synagogue (*Boznica Popera*)
4. Remuh Synagogue
5. Izaak's Synagogue (*Izaka*)
6. Kupa Synagogue
7. Tempel (*Boznica Nowa*)
8. Beth Hamidrash-Emuna
9. New Cemetery
10. Hebrew High School
11. Mikvah

One restricting decree followed another until the Cracow ghetto was established in March 1941 in the Podgorze area. Mass deportation to Belzec took place in the first week of June 1942.

Most of the Jewish points of interest are located in Kazimierz, once a separate Jewish town and now part of Cracow. Kazimierz was established by King Kazimierz Wielki's (Casimir III the Great) charter of 1335. The king's benevolence towards the Jews supposedly was based on his love for a Jewish Girl Esther, who according to the same legend lived at 46 Ulica Krakowska. By 1775, there were about 35 thousand Jews in Kazimierz.

Remuh (Rema) Synagogue, 40 Szeroka (Street), still used for worship. It was built by Rabbi Isserles' father, a banker to King Sigismund II Augustus in 1557, and converted in 1870 by Mateusz Crucci. The name is a contraction of Rabbi Moses Isserles, who preached and taught in this synagogue (Encyclopedia Judaica), or Rama as he is shown in "The Early Achronim."

Old Jewish Cemetery (Kirkut Remuh), adjoining the Remuh (Rema) Synagogue on Szeroka 40 (Street), is the oldest existing Jewish burial ground in Poland, and dates from 1533. It was used between 1552-1800. The only tombstone that has survived virtually unscathed is that of Rabbi Moses Isserles, the sixteenth-century sage and a scholar of Maimonides. The epitaph on Rabbi Isserles' tomb reads: "From Moses to Moses, there was none like Moses." Rabbi Isserles (1510-1572) is remembered particularly for his commentary on the supplement to Joseph Caro's Shulhan Arukh. Part of the cemetery is a wall built from pieces of gravestones destroyed by the Nazis. The synagogue was renovated in the late fifties with the assitance of American Joint.

Some other leaders of the Cracow Jewish community are buried here:

Mordechai Saba,known as Singer, was the head of the Yeshiva from 1572 to 1576.

Natan Nata Spiro (1591-1633), son of the community
leader Rabbbi Solomon. Spiro was head of the Yeshiva

in the years 1617-33. Joel Sirkes (1561-1640), known as Bach and rabbi of the community in the years 1618-1640. He was an authority on the Talmudic Law.

Gershon Saul Yom Tov Lipman Heller (1579-1654), the son of Nathan, he was a leader of communities in Vienna and Prague, and in the years 1643-1654 served as rabbi of the Cracow community. In the years 1648-1654 he also headed the Yeshiva.

Mozes Enzels, son of Naphtali, rabbi of Cracow in the years 1694-1706.

Mordechai Deiches, son of Shimon Nachlis, rabbi of the Cracow community in the seventeenth century.

Izaak Landau, son of Zvi Hirsh, rabbi of the Cracow community in the years 1754-1768.

Izaak Halevy (Halewi), son of Mordechai, rabbi of Cracow community and head of the Yeshiva in the years 1776-1799.

New Jewish Cemetery at 55 Miodowa was established in 1800. It is still used as a Jewish burial place. Its oldest matzevot date back to the ninteenth century.

The cemetery, which was devastated during the occupation was restored thanks to the assitance of the American Joint Distribution Committee. A memorial to the victims of Shoah is located near the entrance. Some of the famous citizens of Cracow are buried here. Among them, Dr. Nussenfeld, director of the Jewish hospital; Maurycy Gottlieb (1856 -1879), one of the best Jewish painters in the world and a student of Polish national painter Jan Matejko; Rabbi Ozjasz Thon, the spiritual leader of the progressive (reform) movement in Cracow and a member of Polish Sejm (parliment); and Maciej Jakobowicz, the past president of the Jewish community in Poland.

A destroyed cemetery at Ulica Jerozolimska.

Mickiewicz Monument on the city's main square (Rynek Glowny) commemorates Adam Mickiewicz, Poland's national poet, who was one of the great champions of Jewish rights in Polish history. His national epic *Pan Tadeusz* was translated into many languages including Hebrew.

The Judaica Branch of the Historical Museum of Cracow is located in the (renovated in 1956) Old Synagogue (Alte Shul-Stara Boznica) in Kazimierz area of Cracow at 24 Szeroka (Street). It contains a collection of Judaica from seventeenth, eighteenth and twentieth centuries. Among the exhibits are works of master jewelers who specialized in Judaica including: Kelmer, Lopienski, Pogorzelski, Reidel, Szekman and Szyldberg. It was erected in the fifteenth century and was modeled on older synagogues in Worms, Regensburg and Prague. After the fire the Synagogue was rebuilt by Matteo Gucci of Florence. During World War II the synagogue was partially destroyed and profaned by the Germans and its courtyard used by Germans for executions. It was rebuilt after the war, mainly due to the efforts of Boleslaw Drobner, a Jewish Sejm (parliament) deputy. The permanent exhibition covers the pre-war history of Kazimierz (the Jewish area of Cracow), as well as the fate of the Jews of Cracow in Plaszow and other death camps. There is a plaque commemorating a visit to the synagogue by Tadeusz Kosciuszko, hero of the Polish uprising against the Russians (and of the American Revolution), who came to call the Jewish population of Cracow to arms (1794). The plaque reads: "The Jews proved to the world that whenever humanity can gain, they would not spare their lives. Here, in the old synagogue, in the days of insurrection of 1794, Tadeusz Kosciuszko called the Jews to arms in the fight for liberation of the country." The president of Poland visited the synagogue in 1931. Here also the famous Rabbi Beer Meisels made patriotic speeches supporting the Polish fights for independence in 1831, 1846 and 1863.

Ulica (Street) Meiselsa is named for Dov Berush Meisels, a mid-nineteenth-century rabbi who served in the senate of the Republic of Cracow as one of the leaders of the Polish liberation movement.

Ulica (Street) Izaka is named after Rabbi Isaac of Prossnitz, who in 1530 founded the first Jewish printing shop in Poland.

Ulica (Street) Joselewicza is named for Colonel Berek

Joselewicz, who commanded a Jewish regiment in Kosciuszko's revolt against the Russians in 1794.

The Jewish Community Building at 2 Skawinska (Street) before the war housed a Jewish library, and now houses a kosher kitchen assisted by Joint (JDC).

Jewish Social and Cultural Association is at 38 Dluga Street.

The Temple, 24 Miodowa (Street), built in 1862, is usually open on major holidays, when the tiny Remu Synagogue cannot hold the worshipers. Originally a progressive (Postepowa) synagogue, now orthodox. Here before world War II the famous Oziarz Thon preached. Near the temple a modern mikvah was constructed. (Pre-war mikvah was located at 6 Szeroka Street).

Poper's Synagogue, located at Szeroka 16, was constructed in 1620 by a rich merchant Wolf (Bocian) Poper; now used as a District Culture Club studio. From the original fixtures, only "Aron Hakodesh" survived. Renovated after the war, it now serves as a youth house.

Boznica Wysoka, high synagogue at Jozefa 38, built in 1556-1563, serves today as reconstruction workshop for works of art.

Izaak's Synagogue (Boznica Izaaka Ajzyka) at Jakuba 25 was built in 1638-1644 by Izaak Jakubowicz, banker to King Wladyslaw IV. The design is that of Francesco Olivieri. It was renovated somewhat after the war and now serves as sculptors' studio. A complete reconstruction is in the process for a possible library use.

Boznica Kupa, at Jonatana Warszauera 8, was built from community funds—the "kupa"-in 1647; before the war used by "Mizrahi"; today used by cooperative.

Sheerit Bnei Emuna synagogue from ninteenth century is located at Ulica Bochenska 4.

Chevrah Tehilim synagogue at Ulica Meiselsa 18 is now used by a dance group.

Beth Hamidrash Kovea Itim L'Tora at 42 Jozefa was built in 1810, and is now used as a residence.

Cafe Cyganeria', a tablet at the Cyganeria Cafe across the street from the municipal theater reads: "On the night between the 24th and 25th of December 1942, a group of soldiers of the People's Army and the Jewish Fighting Organization carried out an operation on the Cyganeria hall, which was full of Germans and inflicted heavy losses upon the conqueror." The operation took place on the night of December 22nd or 24th. All those who took part in it were Jews, led by Adolf Liebeskind and Jehuda Lieber.

Cracow Ghetto

The Cracow ghetto was established on March 13, 1943. The Jewish Combat Organization (Z.O.B.) under the leadership of Dolek Liebeskind, Shimshon Dranger, Heshek Bauminger and Benek Halbreich operated here, too, trying to organize resistance and eliminating informers. A commemorating tablet in honor of the ghetto heros has been placed on the house in which the Jewish Combat Organization had their headquarters. Few survived of the 68,000 Jews closed up in the Cracow ghetto. Most of them were murdered in the camps of Plaszow (near Cracow), Belzec, Sobibor, Majdanek, and Auschwitz-Birkenau. Among those murdered on the way was the great Yiddish poet Mordechai Gebirtig. whose song "S' Brennt" (It Burns) became the anthem of the Jewish resistance.

It Burns

It burns, brothers, it burns
    The time of anguish-God Forbid-now churns
    When the village and you in one blow
    Turns to ashes, to flames all aglow.
    Nothing will remain at all—
    Just a blackened wall—
    And you look and you stand,
    Each with folded hand.

And you look and you stand,
    At burned village and land.

    It burns, brothers, it burns,
    To you alone this agony turns.
    If you love your town, its name,
    Take the vessels, quench the flame.
    Quench it with your own blood too:

Show what you can do.
Brothers, do not look and stand,
Each with folded hand.
Brothers, do not look and stand
While town burns and land.

Andante

Es brent bri - der es brent.___
brent bri - der es brent.___

S'ken cho - li - le ku - men der mo - ment.___
Dos iz nor in aich a - lein ge - vendt.___

Ven dos shte - tl mit aich tzu - za - men
Ven dos shte - tl iz aich ta - ier

zol a - vek mit ash un fla - men
nemt die kei - lim lesht dos fa - ier,

Blai-bn zol a pus-ter shliad shvar-tze pus-te vent.
Lesht mit ai - er ei - gn blut ba vaist vos ihr kent.

Un ihr shteit un kukt a - zoi zich mit far-leig-te
Shteit nit bri - der ot a - zoi zich mit far-leig-te

hent. Un ihr shteit un kukt a-zoi zich vie
hent. Shteit nit bri-der un kukt a-zoi zich vie

un - zer shte - tl brent.
un - zer shte - tl brent.

Es

The Heros of the Ghetto Square (Plac Bohaterow Ghetta 6) marks the spot from which the Jews of Cracow were deported to Auschwitz and Belzec.

Students' house (Dom Akademicki) at Ulica Przemyska 2 provided housing for 140 Jewish students at the Jagiellonian University before the war. It is now used as a student house for the School of Music.

Ritual slaughter house at Plac Nowy 11 is now used as a market hall.

High school at the cross section of Brzozowa Street and Podbrzezie was the center of Jewish education. The Hebrew gymnasium (high school) was located at 8/10 Podbrzezie; the crafts high school at No. 3; primary school at 5 Brzozowa; and "Mizrahi" school at Ulica Miodowa 26. A plaque is located on the building at the intersection. Also Solomon Deiches Beth Hamdrash was located in the same area.

State Children's Home #2, memorial plaque honors Janusz Korczak at Ulica (Street) Chmielewskiego, 6.

Pankewicz Pharmacy, 18 Bohaterow Getta at the "Apteka Pod Orlem" (Pharmacy Under the Eagle) was situated on the border of the Cracow Ghetto and because of its Polish owners has a secret passage from it.

Headquarters of the Jewish Combat Organization (Zydowska Organizacja Bojowa) were located near the Pharmacy at 6 Bohaterow Getta. A commemorative plaque was installed on the wall of the fifth anniversary on the liquidation of the ghetto. One of the leading figueres of Z.O.B. (Jewish Combat Organization) in Cracow was Bernard Halbreich, an N.C.O in the Polish army who was killed in action in February 1943. Now a modest museum with a plaque states that the Jewish Fighting Organization (Zydowska Organizacja Bojowa) was founded there.

Szpitalna Street had shops before the war belonging to Jews who specialized in secondhand books.

62 Grodzka Street housed before the war the Jewish printing press owned by the Jozef Fiszer family. It printed many famous works including those of Ahad Haam, Bialik, Mendel Mocher Sefarim, Shalom Aleichem and others.

Jewish Hospital at 8 Skawinska until World War II was occupied by the Jewish hospital called Israelite Hospital which was built in 1822. The archives found there were transferred to the Jewish Historial Institute in Warsaw. It is now used by the Municipal Medical Department.

Jewish Theater 7 Bochenska Street housed before the war the Jewish Theater. It witnessed such Jewish theatrical talents as the Turkows, Ida Kaminski, Djigan and Shumacher.

Ulica (Street) Berka Joselewicza was named after the Jewish colonel—a hero of the Kosciuszko uprising.

Ulica (Street) Zamenhofa was named after Doctor Ludwik Zamenhof, the father of Esperanto.

Plaszow (near Cracow). See separate listing.

Podgorze, Ulica (Street) Lwowska 25/29 has a plaque on the remains of the wall of the Cracow ghetto which existed from March 3, 1941 - March 14, 1943. The remaining ghetto inhabitants were killed on the spot or sent to death camps in Belzec, Majdanek and Sobibor.

Czechowice-Dziedszice

Monument here honors Jews of this branch of Auschwitz camp shot by the Germans on the eve of liberation on January 19, 1945.

Dabrowa

The synagogue is now a warehouse.

Dabrowa Tarnowska

The Jewish community goes back to the seventeenth century. By 1939 about twenty-five hundred (40 percent) of the population were Jewish. The ghetto was established in the summer of 1940. It was liquidated by deportation to the ghetto of Tarnow, as well as death camp Belzec.

Most of the places of Jewish interest are located at Ulica Berka Joselewicza (the Jewish colonel in the Kosciuszko uprising). They are the synagogue, built in ninteenth century by Abraham Goldstein which is now used as a cultural center; the cemetery with 50 matzevot and two monuments honoring the victims of Shoah and the "Talmud-Tora" school, now used for offices.

Debica (Dembitz)

The synagogue at Krakowska 3 is now a warehouse. The cemetery with 50 remaining matzevot is at Cmentarna. A memorial in the woods of Wolica commemorates 600 Jews of Debica shot by the Germans on July 10, 1942.

Deblin

Obelisk at Ulica (Street) Bieruta commemorates the victims of that branch of Majdanek concentration camp, who worked here at the Heinkel Aeroplane Works.

Drobin

A memorial at the Jewish cemetery of Ulica Sierpecka 54 honors the victims of the Holocaust.

Dubiecko

Mass grave at the Jewish cemetery holds 150 Jews murdered in the years of 1942-43.

Dukla

The synagogue is now a market. Baron Hirsh's school at "Bursa Zydowska" is now a public school.

Dzierzoniow

Congregation and house of worship at Krasickiego 28. The cemetery with some one hundred matzevot is at Wolna 6.

Dzwierzno

Mass grave at the cemetery contains remains of some 1,000 Jewish women from prisons in Bocienie and Szerakopas.

Gdansk (Danzig)

Jewish presence in Gdansk goes back to the 14th century, notwithstanding restrictions imposed on Jews by the German knights (Crusaders) and subsequently Polish kings and the city council. Jewish settlements were definitely established in the city's neighboring villages of Stare Szkoty, Chmielniki and Winnica, and there is even a record of a kosher inn (Zloty Pierscien-Gold Ring).

Today there are remnants of the cemetery at Zydowskiej Gorki (Jewish Hills). The great synagogue at Ujezdzalnia (now Boguslawskiego) was demolished by the Nazis in 1939. Synagogue at Biskupa Gora, Menonitow 2 is now a pentecostal church. Synagogue at Wrzeszcz, Partyzantow 7, is now a music school.

Jewish cemetery between Reformacka, Cmentarna and Browicza streets with one hundred matzevot, the oldest dating back to 1786.

The most significant testimony to the Jewish presence in Gdansk are the paintings by Izaak Van Den Blocke (who died in 1626). They adorn the Gdansk City Hall, and not only deal with biblical scenes, but also show Jewish merchants participating in the commerce of Gdansk.

Gielczyn

Monument in the woods honors twelve thousand people executed by the Germans from mid-1942 to September 1944. Seven thousand of those were Jewish.

Gliniska

A grave holds Jewish families murdered on October 30, 1942.

Gliwice

Gliwice, which was part of Germany before World War II, suffered from Nazi excesses already in the 30s. All the men were deported to Buchenwald in 1938. The cemetery at Na Piasku has 800 remaining matzevot; cemetery at Poniatiowskiego, 400 matzevot. A tablet at 204 Przszynski commemorates victims of a camp in the area.

Congregation and house of worship is at Dolne Waly 9. Synagogue at Dolne Waly 15 is now deserted.

Glogow Malopolski

Three mass graves near the road to Rzeszow mark the spot where the Jews of Rzeszow were shot during the liquidation of the ghetto.

Golub-Dobrzyn

A monument at the Plac (Square) Stulecia honors the inhabitants of the town and the Jewish population who lost their lives. Both cemeteries at Krasickiego and Rypinska were completely destroyed.

Gora Kalwarja (Gur-Ger)

Jews were permitted to settle in this town near Warsaw in 1745. By the eve of World War II, half of its population was Jewish, about 3500. It was known as the "new Jerusalem."

Gerer Rebbe's synagogue at Pijarska, once the seat of a famous Chassidic dynasty of the Alter family, still stands but is now a warehouse and barn. Only the metal framework of a Magen David can still be seen in a circular window high up on the outer wall recalling its original role in Jewish history. What was once the residence of the Gerer Rebbe and the adjacent yeshiva have been converted into tenements. Gerer Rebbe Abraham Mordechai Alter managed to escape from Poland and reached Palestine in 1940.

In the old Jewish cemetery at Kalwaryjska there is a monument to the 5,000 Jews who perished at Gora Kalwaria at the hands of the Nazis.

Gorlice (Gorlitza)

At Ulica Korczaka (named for Janusz Korczak) a tablet marks the location of a camp, where liquidation of the Gorlice ghetto took place. The synagogue at Piekarska 3 is now a bakery. A memorial tablet is on the wall. The synagogue at Dworzysko is now a fire station.

Grodno

Monument remembers Jewish women from Hungary, Romania and Bulgaria who worked at fortifications in what was a branch of Stutthof camp. The camp existed from August 1944 to January 1945.

Grojec

By 1856 nearly seventy percent of the inhabitants of Grojec were Jewish. By 1939, 5200 Jews lived there.

Ghetto was created in July 1940. Some inhabitants were herded to the Warsaw ghetto; the remaining 3000 to Treblinka.

Cemetery near the road to Mszonowa marks the mass grave of victims of extermination in 1943. Rabbi's house next to it was the community house at Ulica Bozniea (Synagogue Street); the house is now used as a living area.

Gross-Rosen (Rogoznica)

Concentration camp located at Kamienna Gora was a branch of Sachsenhausen concentration camp, which initially contained Soviet POWs. It became in May 1941 an independent camp Gross-Rosen. Towards the latter part of 1945 it contained some 84,000 prisoners, but at times, it had as many as 125,000. Some original structures were reconstructed and turned into a museum. Some 40,000 victims were murdered there. Monument and mausoleum honors the victims of the camp. They are constructed of the granite stones dug up by the prisoners. The wall contains earth from branches of the camp.

Monument and mausoleum honor the victims of the camp. The pair were constructed of the granite stones dug up by the prisoners. The wall contains the earth from branches of the camp.

PLAN OF CONCENTRATION CAMP AT GROSS-ROSEN

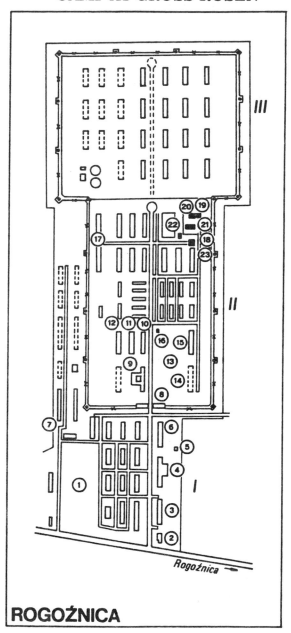

ROGOŹNICA

I. COMMANDANT'S BUILDING
1. Barracks of S.S.
2. Prison
3. Commandant's office
4. S.S. Canteen (presently holding the Museum
5. Dog house
6. Block Fuhrer (Head of the Block)
7. Stores and workshops

II. MAIN CAMP
8. Main gate
9. Admittance office
10. Clothing stores
11. Old baths
12. Storage depots
13. Parade grounds
14. Laundry
15. Kitchen
16. Bell tower
17. Hospital
18. Place of execution
19. Old crematorium
20. Gas chamber
21. Crematorium

Halbow (Krempna Parish)

Mass grave of 1,257 Jews from the area, as well as those brought from Lodz, is here.

Hrubieszow (Rubishov)

At the Jewish cemetery at Ulica (Street) Krucza, there is a monument in memory of 5,700 inhabitants (ten thousand including local Jews) of the ghetto (not closed). It was liquidated in 1942 and its inhabitants deported to Sobibor.

An underground organization was established in 1941 under the command of Arieh Perec (Porecki) and Solomon Brand.

Ilawa

A plaque at the steam engine factory (Lokomotywnia P.K.P.) at Ulica Wojska Polskiego 9 marks the location of the penal work camp. The cemetery at Biskupia was completely devastated.

Ilowa

A memorial tablet is dedicated to the prisoners of the slave labor camp at Ilowa, which was a sub-branch of KL Gross-Rosen.

Inowroclaw

First mention of Jews in Inowroclaw dates back to 1447. At Ulica (Street) Okrezek, a memorial erected in 1975 commemorates victims of the concentration camp at Blonie. The cemetery at Studzienna was destroyed.

Izbica

Tzadik Mordechai Joseph Leiner held his court in Izbica. His son and successor Yaacov Leiner wrote "Beth Yaacov" here.

There were 4000 Jews living in Izbica on the eve of World War II. The last Jews of the town were deported in 1943 to various death camps. The cemetery is nearly destroyed. The Germans executed over four thousand Jews here and they were buried in mass graves. There are graves of victims of the ghetto killed by the Germans in 1941.

Izbica served as a transit point to Belzec and Sobibor not only for the Jews of the area, but also for those brought from Czechoslovakia, Austria, and Germany.

Jagiella-Niechcialki

A monument is to the victims of the two nearby camps, Perlkinie and Wolce Pelkinskie. About eight thousand people, Jews, Gypsies, and Russian POWs are buried here.

Janikowo

A mass grave at the Catholic cemetery contains remains of Jews discovered at the railway tracks (Inowroclaw-Poznan).

Jaroslaw

The synagogue at Opolska 2, which was built in 1807, is now an art school.

Jaslo

The synagogue is now a restaurant. A memorial tablet is in the Krajowicki forest at the mass grave of 260 victims of Nazis shot in July 1942. The cemetery at Florianski has one hundred matzevot.

Jozefow

An obelisk erected in 1974 marks an execution spot of Jews from Poland, Czechoslovakia and Austria.

The synagogue is now a silo.

Katowice

The Jewish community before the war consisted of 8500 members, a number of them having left after the 1937 program. Most of the Jews were forced to leave town in the first few months of the German occupation. A monument is between Mickiewicza and Skargi streets on the location of synagogue destroyed by the Germans.

Jewish community center and house of worship is at Mlynska 13.

The synagogue is now an apartment house.

Kazimierz-upon-Vistula (Kazimierz Dolny [Kuzmir])

In the fifteenth and sixteenth centuries Kazimierz upon Vistula was a place of regional markets from all of the Lublin area. By the ninteenth century the population was mainly Jewish. By March 1942 there were no Jews left in Kazimierz.

There is a synagogue from the early 18th century on Lubelska Street. At present it serves as a cinema, Wisla. A memorial tablet is on the wall.

A small inn is named Esterka after King Kazimierz's supposedly Jewish spouse, Esther.

A monument at the cemetery consisting of broken gravestones creates a "wailing wall" for the victims of the Holocaust. A stone memorial erected by Arie Meler of Canada marks the mass grave commemorating his parents and 500 Jews of Kazimierz and the area murdered in October 1942. The cemetery at Lubelska was completely destroyed. The cemetery at Czerniawa has a few matzevot and a monument. A small collection of Judaica is at the Gold Museum.

Incidentally, Kazimierz is the birthplace of S.L. Szneiderman, who wrote under the pen name A. Lubliner.

Kielce (Keltz)

Kielce is provincial capital in south central Poland. On the eve of War World II, 20 thousand of its 50 thousand inhabitants were Jewish. In 1941 the Kielce Ghetto was established, and existed until May 1943. A tablet is at the synagogue at Rewolucji Pazdziernikowej which is today used as archives. The cemetery at Pakosz Dolny has about 150 matzevot remaining.

In 1927 Dawidek Rubinowicz, author of *The Diary of Dawidek* Rubinowicz, (the Polish equivalent of Anne Frank), was born. The book was first published in Polish in 1960. Rubinowicz perished in Treblinka on September 22, 1942.

The infamous pogrom of July 1946 took place here. Forty two Jews who survived the war were murdered. This event triggered the emigration of some twenty thousand Jews to Palestine in July 1946. Similar events sporadically took place even before the Kielce pogrom. According to a report of the Manchester Guardian, 350 Jews were killed in 1945 after the hostilities had ended. A monument at Planty 7, honoring the victims was erected recently.

MAP OF KIELCE

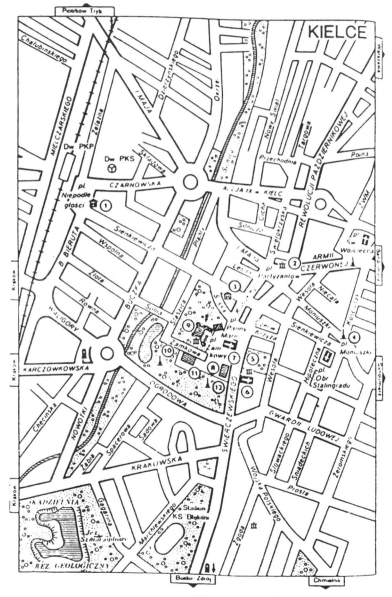

Kock

First signs of the Jewish community dates back to the seventeenth century. Before the war there were about 2500 Jews in Kock. Most of them were murdered by the Germans in August 1942 in Parczew.

Tzadik Mendel of Kock (Menachem Mendel Morgenstern) settled there in 1829, heading an important Chassidic center. In fact he was a teacher of the famous Tzadick of Gora Kalwaria (Gere Rebe).

Ulica (Street) Berka Joselewicza was named after Colonel Berek Joselewicz commander of a Jewish legion, who fought and fell in battle at Kock while fighting the anti-Russian rebellion of General Tadeusz Kosciuszko, a Polish hero of the American revolution.

Ulica (Street) Bojownikow Getta Warszawskiego is a street named to honor the fighters of the Warsaw ghetto.

The cemetery is nearly destroyed, only a few matzevot remain.

Kokoszki

This town was a branch of the Stutthof concentration camp. A pillar commemorates the victims of the camp which was liberated by the Red Army on March 26, 1945.

Kolbuszowa

The synagogue at Piekarska was a wheat silo for some time and is now a museum. The cemetery at Krakowska has mass graves.

Kolce

In the fall of 1943 the Germans formed a forced labor camp for Jews from Poland, Hungary, and Greece. It was transformed in June 1944 into a subcamp of KL Gross-Rosen. The camp was liberated by the Red Army on May 8—9, 1945. A cemetery contains 25 mass graves. Tablets in Hebrew and Polish are at the gate to the cemetery.

Kolo

A stone at Plac (Square) Bahaterow Stalingradu on the

wall of the remains of the synagogue and the Mikva burned in 1939, commemorate Jews from the neighboring camps.

Konin

A tablet at the cross section of Bydgoskiej and Kolejowej (Streets) honors a few hundred Jewish victims of the labor camp.

Remnants of a synagogue also can be seen in Konin.

Koniusz

A memorial stone at the parish cemetery honors a family of seven (including three children) shot on June 22, 1943, for hiding Jews. on June 22, 1943.

Kornick

A ninteenth century Moorish synagogue is located here.

Kosarzyska (Piwniczna County)

A plaque commemorates 19 Poles shot for aiding Jews on September 3, 1943.

Krasnik

The synagogue, which was established in 1637 at Boznicza, is now used as city offices. The cemetery at Podwalna, which was totally destroyed, was rebuilt. The cemetery at Gory still has a few remaining matzevot. A memorial at Bieruta Street honors victims of labor camp (Branch of Majdanek).

Krepa

A grave at the parish cemetery notes a Polish villager and a Jew hidden by him. Both were shot by the Germans in September 1944.

Krepice (Melgiew County)

A memorial is for the victims of mass executions in the woods of Krepiec in the years 1941-1944. A total of 30 thousand from Lublin and Majdanek were shot here (Jews, Poles and Russians).

Krosniewice (Kroshnivitz)

The synagogue is now a cinema.

Krosno

Jews came to Krosno in the fifteenth century. Before the war it had a well established community with 2500 members and some important social institutions such as a loan association, "Gemilat Chesed," and charity organization, "Tomchey Aneeyim".

Most of the Jews of Krosno perished in Belzec in 1942. The cemetery at Ulica Okrzej has 100 remaining matzevot as well as a mass grave of the victims of the Shoah.

Krynki

The Jewish comunity dates back to the seventeenth century. On the eve of the World War II there were 3500 Jews in Krynki with a number of schools, including "Tarbut," and sports clubs, "BarKochba" and "Maccabi." The Germans came to Krynki after the invasion of USSR in 1941. The deportation to Auschwitz took place in July 1943.

The synagogue at Bialostocka is now a cinema. The cemetery, which was established in 1862, has three thousand graves, the oldest dating back to 1750.

Krzeszow

A memorial erected by Charles Schreiber of New York honors 1,500 Jews of Krzeszow murdered in the forest. The cemetery has 50 matzevot remaining, the oldest dating back to 1852.

Kudowa Zdroj

At the St. Catherine Church (Sw. Kateryny), a mass grave notes victims of the sub-branch of KL Gross-Rosen-Sackisch (concentration camp) which imprisoned Jewish girls from Poland, Czechosolvakia and Hungary.

There also was a branch of the Stutthof concentration camp. An obelisk commemorates the victims of the camp which was liberated by the Red Army on March 26, 1945.

Kutery

A monument to the soldiers of the People's Guard led by Stanislaw Olczyk stands here. His partisans and some Jewish families were killed in a skirmish with the Germans on December 6, 1942.

Kutno

The Jewish community in Kutno dates back to the fifteenth century. The town was a known Tora study center as well as of Haskalah movement. They were about nine thousand Jews before World War II. Most of them perished in Chelmno after liquidation of the ghetto in March 1942.

The synagogue is now an office. The cemetery at Spokojna, established in 1793, has a few dozen matzevot remaining.

Lancut

On the eve of the war, 2,800 people (40 percent of the population) were Jewish in this Southeastern town which goes back to the sixteenth century. In the 1930s, as a result of the overall economic situation as well as an economic boycott, the Jewish population was in dire need of and to some degree existed on foreign Jewish aid. By August 1, 1942, there were no Jews left. The famous rabbis of Lancut included Moche Hirsh Melizlich, Moshe Ben Itzhak Eisik and Yaacov Horowitz.

The Lancut synagogue, a masonry building just outside the grounds of the residence of Count Potocki (protector of Jews in that area), survived the war. It was built in 1761. After the war Dr. Stanislaw Balicki convinced the town council not to destroy it, as was its intention, and to create a provincial museum to celebrate Lancut's six hundredth anniversary.

Dr. Balicki wanted to commemorate his murdered Jewish friends by preserving the building. The synagogue was finally restored in 1981 and serves as a regional museum. It is used during the Lancut festival for official ceremonies.

A tablet at the Jewish cemetery at Ulica Traugutta commemorates the Jews of Lancut. There are no matzevot left.

Laslo

A memorial plaque at the Jewish cemetery at Ulica Florjanska honors the victims of the Laslo ghetto.

Lask

The Jewish community was established in the sixteenth century and became an important center of Jewish studies. The famous rabbis of Lask were; Meir Goertz, Moshe Yehuda Lejb and Pinchas Zelig.

There were nearly four thousand Jews in Lask before the war. The ghetto was established in November 1940 and liquidation took place in August 1942 by Nazi criminal Hans Bibow by deportation to Chelmno.

The synagogue is now a fire station. The cemetery at Ulica Mickiewicza was destroyed and the cemetery at Lopatki has only 80 matzevot remaining.

Lasy Kazimierzowskie

A monument here is to 8 thousand Jewish victims of Nazi execution in the woods in October 1941 (see Zagorow).

Leczna (Lentchna)

The first mention of Jews in Leczna dates back to 1501. On the eve of World War II there were 2300 Jewish inhabitants.

A tablet commemorates the victims of the ghetto, a place of deportation of some Slovak and Czech Jews. At the time of the liquidation of the ghetto in September 1943, one thousand inhabitants were shot. The rest were deported to Sobibor.

The synagogue at Ulica Boznicza 19 (Synagogue Street) was built in 1648. It was rebuilt in the 50s and is now used as a museum. There is a tablet on the wall honoring 1046 Jews shot in the years 1940 -1942. The cemetery near the highway is nearly destroyed.

Legnica

The Jewish community dates back to 1301. The Nazis pogrom of 1938 left the town with 200 Jews who were deported in June 1941 to Terezin.

The congregation and synagogue is at Chojnowska 17. The cemetery at Worclawska, which was established in 1837, consists of about 1000 graves.

A memorial honoring the heroes of the Warsaw Ghetto was erected on the twentieth anniversary of the ghetto uprising at Plac (Square) Bohaterow Getta (Heroes of the Ghetto).

Lekawica

A common grave at the parish cemetery notes a Pole and three Jews hidden by him. All were shot by the Germans in 1941.

Lesko

A grave of the victims of the Holocaust stands at the Jewish cemetery.

There is a restored seventeenth century synagogue on Moniuszki Street, presently used as a regional museum. There is an old Jewish cemetery nearby with 2000 well-preserved tombs, some from the sixteenth century.

The Jewish community was exterminated in August 1941 in Zaslawie.

Lesno

An obelisk and commemorative tablets honor 64 Jewish women shot by the Germans in 1945.

Lezachow-Glazyna

A stone marks the place of execution by the Gestapo and the Ukrainian police of 16 people, including six Jews, on August 29, 1941.

Lobez-Swietobrzec

A stone was placed in memory of Lieutenant Alexander Segal, who was killed in action against retreating Germans.

Lodz

On the eve of the war, 250 thousand Jews (out of a total population of 670 thousand) lived in this second largest city of Poland. The community was relatively new and started to develop only in the ninteenth century. Its main occupations were industry and crafts.

Jews came to Lodz relatively late and in 1793 there were only 11 Jews in that city. The reason for that was the fact that the village and subsequently the town belonged to the Kujawy bishops. Eventually Lodz became the second largest Jewish community of Poland.

The ghetto, second established in Poland, was the last one to be liquidated in August 1944, and was ruled dictatorially by M.C. Chaim Rumkowski, "the eldest of the Jews," whose signature even appeared on the ghetto money.

An active synagogue is in the courtyard of Ulica Rewolucji 1905 No. 20 (former Poludniowa). It was built by the family Rajchert and demolished during the war, then renovated in 1989.

Ulica (Street) Berlinska was named for Hirsch Berlinski, one of the heroes of the uprising.

A Jewish Cemetery, Bracka and Zmienna (Streets), has a monument memorializing the 200 thousand Jews from Lodz and neighboring towns who were killed by the Nazis. Only 800 Jews had survived the Nazi occupation when Lodz was liberated on January 19, 1945. The monument stands in the middle of a paved plaza. The inscription in three languages reads: "To the sacred memory of those who perished in the destruction of the great Jewish community of Lodz and the vicinity. They died a martyr's death at the hands of the Hitlerites in the ghettos and concentration camps between 1939 and 1945. Your memory will live forever."

After Warsaw, Lodz had the largest Jewish population in Poland. The Jews made a considerable mark on the spiritual and material face of the town. In Lodz the careers of powerful Jewish industrialists, including Poznanski, Kohn, Kentenberg, Silberstain, Jarocinski, Prussak, Landau, and many others, started.

Today's Jewish cemeteries in Poland are practically the only material evidence of the Jewish past. The Lodz cemetery is rich with monuments containing a great number of individual signs, religious inscriptions and historical messages that emanate from these monuments. Commemorative plaques have been placed in the cemetery to honor the martyrdom of Lodz Jews who perished during the Shoah.

Up until the ninteenth century, Lodz was a small rural town belonging to the Wloclawek Parish. In 1811 the Jewish community bought 1820 square ells of land from the Lipinski family and founded a cemetery there. In the course of time the neighboring grounds were bought and its area was enlarged. In this way the old Jewish cemetery in Wesola Street was established. Today it is at the crossroads of Lutomierska Street and Zachodnia Street. By the end of 1811, a funeral fraternity came into being. The Jews had their own rabbi. His Great Lightness Rabbi Jehuda Arie. The cemetery's present size is 101 acres and together with the building it covers an area of 105.6 acres. The layout of the cemetery was designed in 1913 by A. Zeligson.

During World War I the wooden fence surrounding the cemetery was destroyed. Short of finances to enter upon any larger project, the community protected the cemetery with an earthen wall that was unable to save it from devastation. Only in 1922 could adequate funds be raised and a brick wall was put up within a year. Up util World War II the cemetery attendants numbered 15 to 20 and the place was maintained in perfect order.

During the Nazi occupation the cemetery was within the boundaries of the ghetto. It contained Jews of Lodz, as well as some 20 thousand from Germany, Austria, Czechoslovakia, Holland and Luxembourg. In those tragic days the plots along Bracka Street filled up fast. Starvation, diseases and epidemics decimated the ghetto's population. Between 1940 and 1943, 40,869 victims of the Nazis were buried there. Their graves were called the "Ghetto Field." Also there (in plots P IV and P V) are more than 600 graves of the Gypsies killed by the Nazis or victims of the typhoid epidemics. The common grave of some members of the Polish Resistance is situated by the fence along Kaufman Street.

The Germans did not manage to destroy the cemetery. Up until the very last moment it served as an execution place with pits dug along the internal wall prepared for the last few hundred Jews still in the ghetto. As B. Maliniak has noted "Synagogues and cemeteries seem to be the only really stable and permanent historical monuments to the Jews."

The Lodz synagogues were burnt down by the Nazis; the cemetery survived as the largest in Europe, with more than 180 thousand existing monuments. Most of them are traditional matzevot, with elaborate symbolic reliefs in the upper parts of the states. Underneath there are epitaphs unique inscriptions in a square writing. They contain traditional abbreviations, characteristic phrases, and biblical quotations. Some epitaphs, in the eighteenth-century style, are considerably long, often forming an acrostic. On some matzevot, a prayer for the dead is carved at the back. Apart from the matzevot, a large number of modern monuments, family graves (including the parents of Arthur Rubinstein and Julian Tuwim), and mausolea (the most striking belonging to the Poznanski family) are to be found in the cemetery concentrated mainly in the plot along the main alley. Most styles from the turn of the nineteenth and early twentieth centuries are to be found there: Modernism, Art Nouveau, Neoclassicism, and other styles. They were made famous by masters such as, Hersz Hirszberg, Abraham Ostrzega, Otto Rycher from Berlin, H. Broder, L. Pasmanik and many others. In 1975, some 100 tombstones and monuments were included in the Historical Monuments Register of the City of Lodz; in 1980, the whole cemetery was declared an historical monument.

Ulica (street) Juliana Tuwima was named after Julian Tuwim, a famous Polish Jewish poet. There is also a youth palace named after him (at Moniuszki 4A), as well as a theater, Theatr Studyjny (at Kopernika 8).

Lodz Philharmonic (Filharmonia), located at Narutowicza 20, is named after Arthur Rubinstein.

Jewish People's Library, 32 Wieckowskiego (Street), houses the Jewish Social and Cultural Association.

Jewish State Theater Building, 15 Wieckowskiego (Street), was erected in 1951 on the ruins of the Jewish Scala Theater. It is now used for general theatrical purposes since the Jewish Theater moved its activities to Warsaw (Teatr Nowy [New theater], at 93 Zachodnia).

MAP OF LODZ

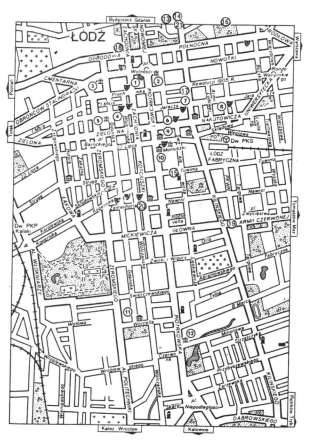

4 - "Teatr Nowy (former Yiddish Theater   14 - Berlinski Street   18 - Poznanski House
   named after Arthur Rubinstein)   15 - Julian Tuwim Street   19 - Janusz Korczak Hospital
6 - Lodz Philharmonic   16 - Jewish Cemetery   20 - Zamehoff Street
13 - Berek Joselewicz Street   17- Synagogue   21 - Heros of the Ghetto Uprisi

Synagogue in the courtyard of apartment building at Ulica Piotrkowska 114/116. Used after the war as a printing house and storage is presently being renovated.

Peretz Playground is named after Yitzhak Leib Peretz, the Yiddish writer.

A plaque on the building at Ulica Kimanowskiego, which

housed the Gestapo headquarters, commemorates the victims of the ghetto (and the Gypsies).

Poznanski Textile Works (1875), owned by the Poznanski Textile Magnates (see mausoleum a the Lodz cemetery), is at Ogrodowa 17 (today's LZPB)

Korczak's Hospital at Armi Czerwonej 15 and Nowa 30 is named after Janusz Korczak.

Lomazy

Mass grave of two thousand Jews murdered during the liquidation of the ghetto is here.

Lomza

There were 737 Jews in Lomza in the beginning of the 19th century. The community had a synagogue, two Yeshivot and newspapers, *Lomsher Shtyme* and *Lomsher Lebn*. Both Agudat Israel and Bund were active in town.

By 1939 there were 11 thousand Jews in town. The ghetto was established on August 12, 1941 and liquidated by deportation to Auschwitz in November 1942.

Memorial stone at Ulica Zambrowska marks the mass grave of victims of German executions in 1941-1943.

Cemeteries at Ulica Rybki and Ulica Waska 69 both were established in 19th century and each have over 150 matzevot.

Obelisk at the Jewish cemetery at Waska Street commemorates the victims of mass murders in the years 1941-1943.

A memorial tablet on the location of a synagogue burned by the Germans in September 1939 honors nine thousand Jews of the town.

Lowicz

Jewish population of Lowicz was forty-five thousand. It had its synagogue and cemetery as well as weekly *Mazowsher Wochenblat*. The inhabitants of the ghetto were deported to the Warsaw ghetto.

Cemetery at Ulica-Leczycka was established in 1830 and still has 200 matzevot.

Synagogue built in 1897 at Ulica Browarna 10 is now used by municipal offices.

Lubaczow

First Jews came to Lubaczow in 1498.

Some famous rabbis taught in Lubaczow among them Hersh Elimelech and Shmuel Nachum Gassenbauer.

Baron Edmond de Rothschild funded the rebuilding of the synagogue in 1899.

Most of the 2500 Jews of Lubaczow perished in Sobibor and Belzec.

Some Jewish partisan units fought in the area under the command of Mietek Gruber and Samuel Jegier.

The synagogue is now a warehouse.

Lublin

Before World War II, forty thousand of the 122 thousand inhabitants of Lublin were Jews, a good number of them employed as grain merchants. Lublin was an important center of the Zionist Movement and all Jewish political parties were active there. The Jewish population centered around the Podzamcze area (below the castle), mainly Podzamcze, Zamkowa, Krawiecka and Szeroka (known as Jewish Street). The educational establishments included the Tarbut high school, Talmud Tora, Beth Yaacov, and Yavneh schools.

The ghetto was established in March 1941. The bulk of the Lublin Jewry perished in Belzec. The rest in Majdan Tatarski and Majdanek.

Lublin was an extremely important center of Torah learning and often was referred to as the "Jerusalem of Poland." In the sixteenth century the first Hebrew printing press in Poland was established (based on the King's Privilege) and the first Talmud printed. The most famous was the one established by Klonimus in 1578. Lublin with its large Jewish population dating from 1336, and indeed the seat of the Council of Four Lands (Va'ad Arba Aratzot), had a number of famous synagogues, including Maharshal Synagogue (built in 1567), said to hold 3,000 worshipers; next to it Maharam Synagogue and Saul Wahl (Prochwownik) Synagogue, named after a man who according to a legend was king of Poland for a day. None survived. In fact both Maharshal and Maharam synagogues survived the war in a devastated form, but were wrecked by orders of the municipal authorities.

Some famous Torah scholars hail from Lublin: among them Rabbi Salomon Szachna, the founder of the Talmudic Yeshiva in the 16th century; Rabbi Maharshal; Hurwitz Maharam Gedalia Meir); Yaacov Itzhav Hurvitz Choze of Lublin (Seer of Lublin), buried at Lublin cemetery. Other famous scholars also came from Lublin. Among them was: Emil Majerson, the philosopher; Zalkind Hurwitz,known as "le Juif de Lublin;" Malwina Majerson,the writer; and physicians: Montallo, Vitalis, and Maj. Also Shalom Baruch Nisenabum, the historian; writer Anna Langfus and Bela Szapiro of the Bund movement; Bela Dobrzycka, the Zionist activist; Moshe Szulsztajn, the poet; Bela Mandelsberg and Szyldkraut, the historian; and Symcha Trachter, the painter.

There is a **Jewish Community Center** and house of worship at Lubartowska 10.

Jewish Cemetery at Ulica (Street) Sienna and Kalinowszczyzna, contains a tablet honoring the victims of terror. The area of the cemetery was used by the Germans as a site for frequent executions. **Martyrs' Memorial**, at Ulica (Street) Sawicka, a monument to the 46 thousand Lublin Jews and more than 250 thousand from other places murdered by the Nazis, is in the heart of the city's new section near the old royal castle. At the base of the monument are buried urns containing ashes of Jews killed at the death camps of Sobibor, Piniatow, Kremplece, Belzec and Zamosc. The monument, a bronze statue, bears an inscription in Polish and Yiddish: "I seek my dear ones in every handful of ashes." The monument stands on the grounds of what was the ghetto during the Nazi occupation. From this spot Jewish deportees from many countries were assembled before being sent to the nearby concentration camps and extermination centers at Majdanek, Plaski, Leipowa, and Sobibor. The old Jewish quarter, established in the early sixteenth century around the castle, was destroyed by the Nazis. The portal that led to the Jewish quarter was known as Jews' Gate. At nearby 19 Szeroka St. was the house in which the Council of the Four Lands (Va'ad Arba

MAP OF LUBLIN

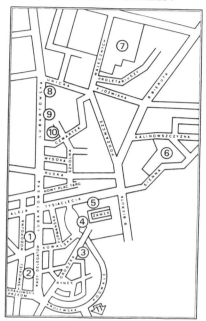

1 - Hall of Remembrance (founded on 9 November 1987)
2 - Monument to the Martyred Jews of Lublin at the Ghetto Victims (unveiled on 9 November 1963)
3 - A Plaque at the Building of the Former "Ochronka" (Orphanage) and Home for the Aged
4 - Memorial Plaque showing the Former Jewish Quarter of Lublin
5 - Memorial Plaque at the Site of the Maharshal and Maharam Synagogues
6 - Old Jewish Cemetery (founded in 1541)
7 - New Jewish Cemetery (founded in 1829(
8 - Building of Yeshivat Chachmey Lublin (Rabbinical Academy) presently the Medical School
9 - Former Jewish Hospital
10 - I. L. Perec House of Jewish Culture (Memorial Plaque)
11 - Majdanek Camp

Aratzot) met annually during the sixteenth and seventeenth centuries.

Synagogue [Chevrat Hanoseem], active whenever minyan can be found, is located on the second floor of an apartment building at Lubartowska 2.

Droga Meczennikow Majdanka (Road of the Martyrs

Gravestones and inscriptions from the Jewish cemetery in Lublin.

of Majdanek) bears a plaque commemorating the martyrs of Majdanek, and is located on the road leading from the railway to the camp.

Jewish Cemetery contains the graves of many eminent rabbinic authorities including those of Solomon Luria (1501-1573, known as "Maharshal") and Rabbi Meir Lublin (1558-1616, known as "Maharam"). The caterer Jozef Honig lives across the street at Dembowskiego 4-17 *(see next page)*.

Jewish Hospital (where author's father worked) at Lubartowska 81 serves as a medical facility.

In the beginning of the twentieth century, Rabbi Meir Shapiro established **Yeshivat Hachamei Lublin**, the largest Yeshiva in Poland, where 400 students studied at any

PLAN OF THE OLD JEWISH CEMETERY

1. Jakow ben Jehuda Halewi Kopelman
2. Hana bat MA
3. Abraham ben Uszaja
4. Jakow Icchak
5. Szloma ben Dawid
6. Jekutiel Zalman
7. Ischar Ber (?)
8. Abraham ben Jakow Iccak Hurwic
9. Miriam bat Szymszon
10. Josef ben Zacharia Mendel
11. Sara Fajga bat Szaul
12. Jehuda Lajib
13. Szalom Szachne ben Josef
14. Dawid Tewi (?) ben Josef
15. Eliezer Lipman (ben Mosze Segal) (?)
16. Jehosza Falk
17. Sara bat Dawid
18. Efraim ben Josef
19. Jakow Dawid ben Mosze
20. Ita bat Menasze Icchak
21. Jehuda bat Mosze Zew
22. Icchak Ajzyk
23. Malka bat Lajb
24. Mosze ben Jehuda
25. Meir ben Meir
26. Heszil ben Jakow
27. Jehuda Lajb ben Meir Aszkenazy
28. Szloma Luria Maharszal
29. Szaul ben Chaim Dawid
30. Jakow ben Efraim Naftali Hirsz
31. Cwi Hirsz ben Zacharia Mendel
32. Meir (?)
33. Natanal ben Meszulam
34. Cwi Hirsz ben Mosze
35. Jakow ben Szmuel
36. Szloma Dawid (Doktor?)
37. Jenta Pesa bar Meir
38. Lea bat Mosze meJanow
39. Zisel bat Szloma
40. Miriam bat Szymon

given time. It is now occupied by the Lublin University School of Medicine Collegium Maius. A former synagogue on the second floor is used as the university's auditorium.

Lublin Castle displays the newly restored painting *Admission of the Jews to Poland* by Jan Matejko, famous Polish painter of many monumental scenes of Polish history. The painting was commissioned in 1889 by Vienna jurist Dr. Arnold Rappaport. It was presumed lost during the war, but it turned up in the spring of 1967.

New Jewish Cemetery at Ulica (Street) Walecznych bears graves of the victims of the Holocaust from the years 1941-1942.

There is a monument marking the grave of Rabbi Shapiro, the founder of the Yeshiva. His remains were reinterred in Jerusalem after the war.

Old Age Home at Ulica Grodzka has commemorative tablet.

People's Home at Ulica named after Perec. Commemorative tablet on the wall.

Lubon

Monument is at a location of a labor camp for Jews (1941-1943) working on the Berlin Warsaw railway.

Lutowisko

A memorial erected in 1969 commemorates 650 Jews and Gypsies shot near the village Catholic church in 1943.

Cemetery has some 400 graves.

Majdanek (Lublin)

Majdanek Concentration Camp established in November 1941, today is really part of Lublin, and has been preserved by the Polish government as a monument. Here, between 120 thousand and 200 thousand Jews from the ghettos of Warsaw and Lublin perished. The memorial is a huge mound of ashes from the bones of the victims. The barracks and gas chambers have been preserved. At the entrance a huge monument in the form of a gate designed by Viktor Tolkin and Janusz Dembek has a vague menorah symbolism.

On November 3, 1943, nearly 19 thousand Jews were shot

MAP OF MAJDANEK CAMP

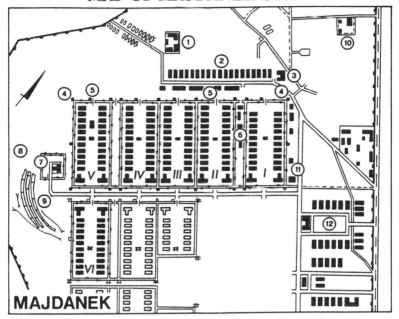

1. Dog's house
2. Stores
3. Baths and gas chambers
4. Watchtowers
5. Watch house
6. Old crematorium
7. New crematorium
8. Area of mass executions
9. Mass execution pits
10. Commandant's house
11. S.S. women quarters
12. S.S. quarters and commandant's offices
I - IV. Barracks

in the camp. The Germans used the euphemism Ernfest (Harvest) for this crime.

Makow Mazowiecki

Jewish community dates back to the middle of 16th century and by 1827 constituted 90% of the population.

The roots of Leon Blum, premier of France, go to Makow. On eve of World War II there were 3500 Jews in Makow. The Germans established ghetto in September 1941. Its inhabitants were deported to Treblinka in the end of 1942.

Synagogue at Zielony Rynek 5 was devastated and rebuilt after the war for apartments.

Mikva at Ulica Przasnyska 19 is now used as a garage.

A monument to the victims of the Holocaust was erected in 1987 from broken matzevot on the grounds of the destroyed cemetery near the railway station.

On the site of the Jewish cemetery a memorial built from broken matzevot (some from the ninteenth century) erected in December 1947.

Malki

Monument stands for some Jewish women murdered here in January 1945.

Miedzyrzec Podlaski

The community was established in the 16th century; it had before the war a synagogue and a number of houses of worship. A memorial at the Jewish cemetery at Ulica (Street) Brzeska 60 commemorates ten thousand Jews of the area.

Miedzyrzec

Neoclassical ninteenth century synagogue at Piotra Skargi Cemetery at Waszkiewicza completely destroyed.

Mielec-Borek (Melitz)

An obelisk at the Jewish cemetery at Ulica Traugutta commemorates one thousand Jews from the area shot by the Germans on March 9, 1942, during the liquidation of the ghetto.

Monument at the Town Square corner Lelewela errected on the spot where the Germans burned the synagogue with the worshipers inside.

Minsk Mazowiecki (Novomintz)

Jews settled here in the first part of the 19th century. It

was a stronghold of the Chassidic movement known for the court of Tzadik Yaacov Perlow.

They were nearly six thousand Jews in Minsk Mazowiecki before the war. The ghetto was established in 1940 and also Jews of Lipno, Pabianice and Kalisz were herded there. After mass executions on August 21, 1942, most of the inhabitants were deported to Treblinka.

Commemerative tablet on the school building on Ulica Siennicka honors 200 victims of atrocity when Germans burned the building.

Monument at Minsk Jewish Cemetery

A monument honoring the 5,500 victims of the Holocaust was erected in 1965 on the location of the Jewish cemetery, Ulica (Street) Dabrowka.

Myslenice (near Cracow)

An obelisk at the Jewish cemetery at Ulica (Street) Tarnowa commemorates the Jews of Myslenice who were deported to the death camps on August 22, 1942.

Nekla

Obelisk at the rail tracks from Nekla to Giecz marks the location of the Julag (Camp for Jews) who worked on the Poznan-Warsaw rail tracks. Grave of 180 Jews in the Catholic cemetery.

Nielisz

Memorial honors victims of the German terror in 1943. Thirty-nine Jews were murdered on this spot.

Niskie Brodno

Obelisk at Lake Niskie Brodno near Brodnica honors Jewish women who worked and perished in the nearby camp. The remains were exhumed after the war from the mass graves and interred at the Military Cemetery of Bydgoszcz.

Nowa Huta

The Youth Culture House is at Osiedle Zgody 13 and has a plaque commemorating Janusz Korczak.

Nowa Wies

Obelisk in the woods near the road to Zapole marks the spot of the mass execution of 250 Jews in 1942. The bodies were transferred in 1951 to the Jewish cemetery in Kolbuszowa.

Nowy Sacz (Neisantz)

First mention of Jews goes back to 1409. In the 19th century Tzadik Chaim Ben Arieh Lejb Halberstam held his court in town. Before World War II there were 150 thousand Jews in Nowy Targ and the outlying areas. The ghetto was established in August 1941. A year later its occupants were deported to Belzec.

At the Jewish cemetery at Ulica Rybacka, a plaque commemorates places of mass executions at Przetakowka cemetery. Some 25 thousand people are buried there. There also is an abandoned synagogue.

Nowy Targ (Neumarkt)

There is a tablet at the Jewish cemetery at Ulica Strzelnicza (Jana Pawla II) where 2,900 Jews of Nowy Targ were executed.

Home of worship at Szaflarska 19 today is used as mechanic's shop.

Nowy Wisnicz

Jews were invited to settle in Nowy Wisnicz by Count Ludomirski in 1606.

The Jewish population of 1000 was deported to Belzec in the summer of 1942.

Cemetery near the road to Limanow features about 300 matzevot. The cemetery was cleaned up and fenced in the 80s.

Olsztyn

Jewish community of Olsztyn goes back to the later part of the 18th century. Erich Mendelsohn, the famous architect was born here in 1897 at Ulica Staromiejska 8.

As the town was part of The Third Reich before the war the persecution of Jews started in the 30s and the Yellow Star was introduced in 1938.

Cemetery at Ulica Zyndrama z Maszkowic is destroyed and now used as a park.

Synagogue at Ulica Kollataja 16 is now a residence.

Opoczno

History of Jews of Opoczno goes back to the reign of Casimir the Great whose supposed love for "Esterka" (Esther) led to a legend that her house is located in this town.

The ghetto established in 1940 was liquidated in October 1942 and its inhabitants deported to Treblinka. A Jewish partisan unit fought in the neighboring forest under the command of Kaniowski (Julian Ajzenman).

A mass grave holds the Jews shot by the Germans at the military cemetery in 1943 (exhumed in June 1967).

Eighteenth century synagogue today used as a cinema.

Orla

Eighteenth century synagogue is now a warehouse.

Osowa

A memorial commemorates the inmates of the labor camp established in 1941. The camp was liquidated in 1943 and its inmates were deported to Sobibor death camp.

Ostroleka

Cemetery at Stefczyka is completely destroyed. The bulk of Jews were deported by the Germans to the Soviet-occupied part of Poland in 1939.

The synagogue is now a garage.

Ostrowiec Swietokrzyski

The community goes back to the 17th century. By the outbreak of World War II 50 percent of the population was Jewish. The last Jews were deported to Auschwitz on 3 August 1944. A resistance group was active in the ghetto under the leadership of David Kempinski, Moshe Stein and the Kopel brothers.

Cemetery at Sienkiewicza has some 200 gravestones including that of Tzadik Meier Halewi Halsztok.

Ostrow Mazowiecki

The cemetery at Broniewskiego is completely destroyed. The bulk of Jews were deported by the Germans to the Soviet-occupied part of Poland in 1939.

Marker in the woods near Ostrow Mazowiecki-Wyszkow road notes the murder of 600 Jews on September 11, 1939.

Oswiecim

In the town of Oswiecim in southwest Poland (near the Auschwitz death camp), there is a Jewish cemetery between Dobrowskiego and Wysokie Brzegi streets. There are about 1000 graves. The cemetery was cleaned up in 1980.

The first Jews arrived in Oswiecim in 1564. On the eve of World War II, 33 percent (4 thousand out of 12 thousand) of the inhabitants were Jewish.

Synagogue at Berka Joselewicza (named after a Jewish Colonel)is used today as residence.

Otwock

A monument at Reymonta marks the spot where the Germans shot 1,500 Jews from the Otwock ghetto between August 19-20, 1942.

New cemetery with 200 gravestones is in a very dilapidated condition.

Ozarow

Cemetery here.

Palmiry

A mass grave, now a cemetery, memorializes the spot in the woods of Kampinow near Warsaw where 1,700 people were executed in January 1940. At least 250 of those murdered were Jewish.

The Woods of Kampinow

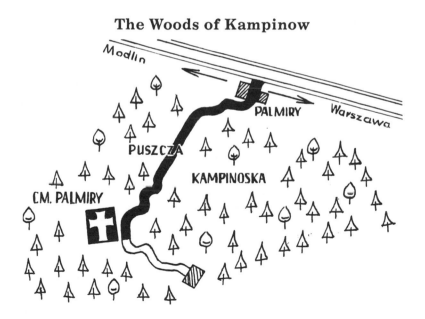

Parczew (Partzeva)

Synagogue at Piwonia is presently a cinema.
Synagogue at Zabia is now a kindergarten.
Cemetery completely destroyed.

A Jewish partisan unit under the command of Alexander Skotnicki was formed here from the Jews who managed to escape from a train to Treblinka.

A memorial at the municipal park commemorates 100 Jewish POWs shot by the Germans on September 18, 1939. There is, however, no mention of their Jewish origin.

Pieszyce

Near the road to Dzierzoniowa a stone commemorates the Warsaw ghetto uprising. It was unveiled on the twentieth anniversary of the uprising April 19, 1963.

There is a monument at the Langenbielan I branch of the concentration camp Gross-Rosen. The branch contained 1,500 prisoners, Jews from Hungary and Slovakia. The camp was liberated on May 8, 1945. The inscription is in Polish and Yiddish.

Pietkowiec (Wadowice Gorne Parish)

A tablet on the school building marks the spot where a family of five was murdered.

Pilzno

There were about 700 Jews in Pilzno before the war.

A grave at the parish cemetery is for Jan Bobowski, murdered by the Germans on April 24, 1943, for helping the Jews. A monument at the Jewish cemetery at Skarpy honors Jews of Pilzno and the surrounding area who were murdered by the Nazis.

The community was established in the sixteenth century. There were 3,500 Jews on the eve of World War II. During the deportation to Treblinka in August 1942, some Jews escaped to the neighboring forests and formed partisan units under command of Zalman Fajnsztat and Michal Majtek.

Pinczow

There is a sixteenth-century Renaissance synagogue at Ulica Klasztorna, which is now being renovated for possible use as a museum.

Both cemeteries at Ulica Batalionow Chlopskich and Slabska are completely destroyed.

MAP OF PINCZOW

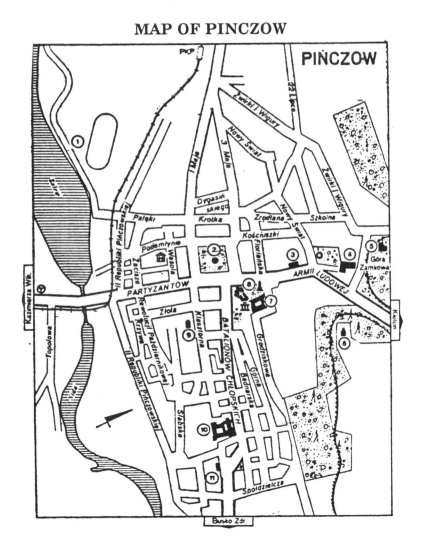

Piotrkow Trybunalski (Petrikov)

The community goes back to the sixteenth century. King Jan Sobieski III, hero of the battle of Vienna granted the Jews the rights to settle in Piotrkow in 1679. On the eve of the war, there were over 10 thousand Jews in Piotrkow.

The labor camps in the area were liquidated in November 1944, and the survivors deported to Rawensbruck and Buchenwald concentration camps, as well as arms factories in Czechoslovakia.

The Jewish cemetery at Ulica Spacerowa was devastated by the Germans who used the cemetery for mass executions of the inhabitants of the ghetto, which was the first set up by the Germans in Poland. A symbolic grave commemorates the victims. The best known mass execution took place on August 14, 1942.

The synagogue is now a library.

The "Duza" (Big) synagogue was rebuilt in 1964, and is now used as a library. The cemetery at Ulica Wojska Polskiego was completely destroyed.

Plaszow (near Cracow)

The concentration camp near Cracow was established in December 1942 on the territory of the Jewish cemetery. This was the last camp established in Poland. One hundred fifty thousand people passed through the camp during its existence. Some eighty thousand people lost their lives there. The camp was liquidated in the fall of 1944.

The monument on the premises of the former concentration camp in Plaszow near Cracow was designed by Ryszard Szczypczynski and Witold Ceckiewicz.

Plock

Cemetery at Ulica 3 Maja was completely destroyed.

On the eve of World War II, the Jewish community comprised 10 thousand souls (about 30 percent of the population).

Some of the famous citizens of Plock were Leib Margulies, the "Mitnaged" (to the Chassidic movement), Shalom Ash, Fish Zilberman and Yakov Warszawski.

The old Synagogue (Dawna Synagogue) at J. Kwiatka 7,

MAP OF PIOTRKOW TRYBUNALSKI

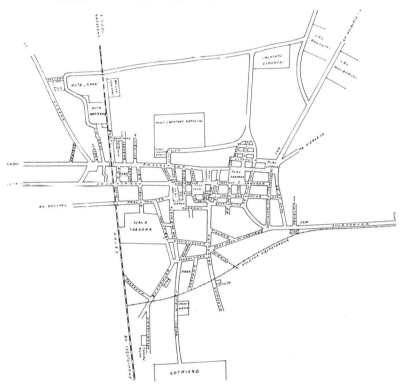

is a classic building from 1810 rebuilt in the twentieth century. It is now used as a cooperative.

The Jewish cemetery at Ulica Sportowa has a memorial honoring Jews of Plock who perished in Treblinka, Sobibor, Belzec and Auschwitz. It was rebuilt in 1980.

Plonsk

Jews came to Plonsk in the 15th century. By the beginning of the 20th century 64 percent of the population was Jewish,about 8,400 on the eve of World WarII.

The ghetto was established in May 1940 and liquidated at the end of 1942 by deportation to Auschwitz.

The most famous citizen of Plonsk was David Ben-Gurion, Israel's first prime minister, who was born here in

MAP OF PLOCK

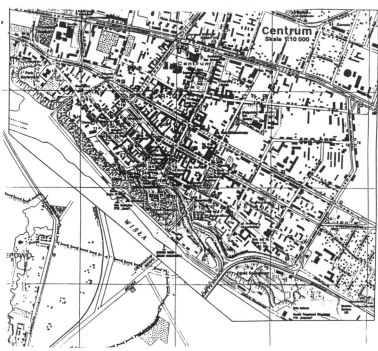

1886. There is a monument in his honor, which was erected on the 100th anniversary of his birth.

Memorial to victims of Shoah are on the grounds of the destroyed cemetery at Ulica Warszawska.

Pniewo

A plaque marks mass grave of Jews and some members of the Home Army from Rutki who were shot in the years 1941-1943.

Pokibry

A plaque at the road to Malce commemorates 106 Jewish inhabitants of Cichanowiec shot by the German gendarmes on December 2, 1942.

Polko (Czorzsztyn County)

There is a grave of five Jews shot in 1943.

Poloniec

Mass graves are in the Jewish cemetery.

Poniatowa

Originally a POW camp for the Russians, this became a concentration camp for Jews from Opole Lubelskie at the end of 1942. In April and May 1943 transports of Jews from the Warsaw ghetto were brought here. On September 3, 1943, the Germans shot 18 thousand prisoners and liquidated the camp.

Poniatowo

Trawniki Concentration Camp Memorial stands in the forest outside this village over a mass grave, and in the village itself. A third and much larger monument is being planned.

Poznan

The community dates back to 1379.

During the division of Poland before World War I, Poznan was under German rule. As a result the "Maskilim" movement was strong (under leadership of David Caro), and Jewish education under strong German influence.

On the eve of World War II there were 1500 Jews in Poznan. By the end of 1939 there were no Jews left.

Cemetery at Ulica Glogowska was completely destroyed and is part of the Poznan fairgrounds.

Synagogue at Wroniecka was used by the Germans as a swimming pool, and is in use as such today.

Section 5 (Kwatera) at the communal cemetery contains a mass grave of hundreds of Jews killed during the German occupation.

Pruszca Golanski

A branch of Stutthof concentration camp, located near the railway station, contained 300 Jewish women prisoners. A monument commemorates the victims.

Przasnysz

A memorial at the Jewish cemetery at Leszno bears the inscription, "In memory of those who lived amongst us."

Przemysl

The first mention of Jews in Przemysl dates to the 12th century. Before World War II the community was comprised of 20 thousand Jews. It was known for its lively political activities, including Folkspartai, Agudat Israel and Bund.

The Soviets, under whose jurisdiction Przemysl was in 1939-40, deported some 7000 to camps and gulags, "inadvertantly" saving some Jewish lives. Those that remained perished in Belzec and Auschwitz.

A memorial tablet unveiled in July 1956 at Ulica Kopernika 14 marks the execution place of two thousand Jews from the Przemysl getto.

At the main cemetery with 200 matzevot on Ulica Slowackiego, there is also a grave of a Jewish woman and child, as wekk as the three women hiding them, all of who were shot by the Germans (Kwatera XIX). There are also 12 mass graves of the victims of Shoah. Cemetery at Rakoczego completely destroyed.

A ninteenth-century synagogue near Wyczoklowskie and 3 Maja streets, is now an art gallery.

Monument near Kunkowce honors the victims of German executions.

Przewrotne

A monument honors the partisans of the area, who also took in some Jews.

Przyrow

Jewish community center and house of worship is at Wlodkowicza 9.

Cemetery at Cmentarna was nearly destroyed.

Przysucha

There is an eighteenth-century synagogue built in 1777.

Pulawy

There were 3600 Jews in Pulawy before the war. The community, which goes back to the 19th century, had a number of institutions including a bank, schools and trade unions. Political parties such as Agudat Israel, Poalei Zion and Bund were active there.

The ghetto was already established in October 1939. Its inhabitants were deported to Opole Lubelskie and at a later stage to Sobibor death camp.

Memorial on the place of the destroyed synagogue honors the Jews of Pulawy. It was unveiled on August 27, 1987, as a result of initiative of Mrs. J. Haubenstock.

Both cemeteries at Ulica Konskowa and Ulica Wlostowica are destroyed.

Pultusk

In September 1939 the Germans deported most of the Jews to the Soviet part of occupied Poland. The cemetery was completely destroyed. A memorial to the victims of Shoah is at 27 Kotlarska Street.

Pustkow

There is a mausoleum at the location of the death camps, which existed here from November 8, 1940, to August 23, 1944. About 16 thousand people lost their lives here, mainly Jews, but also some Poles and Russian POWs. The monument was unveiled on September 6, 1964.

Pyskowice

Cemetery with over 200 graves at Ulica Zadszyny 12. Remnants of 1822 synagogue.

Rabka

The synagogue is now a house.

Monument in the forest near Sloneczna Street over the mass graves of victims of the Nazis.

Rachow-Lipka

A monument honors the Jews of Rachow who worked in

Memorial at Pustkow Death Camp

the mines. On October 3, 1943, all of them were murdered by the Germans.

Radom

The Jewish community dates back to the sixteenth century. It had many Jewish institutions including a hospital, Yeshiva, a few libraries and a number of newpapers in Yiddish and one in Polish (*Trybuna*). Before World War II, the community was comprised of 30 thousand people; the ghetto was established in March 1941. Most of the inhabitants perished in Treblinka (28,000) and Auschwitz.

The well known citizens of Radom included Rabbi Shmuel Mohliver and Simha Treistman.

A monument designed by Jacob Zajdensznir at Ulica Bozniczna (Synagogue Street) near Anielewicza, is named after the hero of the Warsaw ghetto uprising, and honors 33 thousand of the Radom ghetto, which was established in March 1941. Most of the Jews of Radom perished in Auschwitz and Treblinka.

Mass graves at the Jewish cemetery at Ulica Towarowa mark the spot where 20 thousand people were deported during the night of August 16 and 17, 1942. Patients of the Jewish hospital and people from the home for the elderly, some 1,000 in all, were killed on the spot.

Radomsko

Out of 25,000 inhabitants of Radomsko, 9,200 were Jewish. The community enjoyed a rich political life including Bund, and Poalei Zion. It had a Yeshiva and in the 1930s also Hachshara Kibbutz. There was also a high school, private school and Hakoach sports club.

During October 1942 a deportation to Treblinka took place.

There were some Jewish partisan units under command of the Szabatowski brothers, Roza Szapiro and Tuviah Borzykowski.

The Jewish cemetery at Ulica Swierczewskiego was used for mass executions from 1940-1943. During liquidation of the Radomsko ghetto in January 1943, some 1,500 people were shot. There is a commemorative tablet on one of the mass graves.

Radomysl Wielki (Radomishla)

The community goes to the very beginning of seventeenth century. It was an important center of Tora learning. The famous *tzadikim* of Radomysl were Shmuel Engel and Abraham Chaim Horowitz.

By 1939 there were 1,300 Jews in town. Most of them perished in Belzec.

The cemetery near the road to Dabrowka Wislocka features a memorial tablet erected in 1987.

There are still 50 matezvot left, also mass graves of victims of the Shoah shot by the Germans in the summer of 1942.

Judaica "mini" museum at Ulica Kosciuszki 2.

Radymno

The synagogue is now a factory.
The cemetery was totally destroyed. A memorial stone at the cemetery honors 100 Jews shot at the spot in the fall of 1942.

Radzilow (Rodzilova)

There is a marker on the mass grave of 800 Jews shot and burned alive in a barn in August 1941. The cemetery was totally destroyed.

Ratowice

There is a monument to the victims of the concentration camp at Ratowice, where some Polish Jews were imprisoned. The monument was erected in 1967.

Ropica Gorna

An obelisk marks a grave of three Jews shot by the German gendarmes in March 1942.

Rzepiennik Strzyzewski

A mass grave in the woods of Deby marks the place of execution for 364 Jews of Gorlice who were murdered on August 11, 1942. The cemetery with 100 matzevot is near Gromnik-Biecz road.

Rzeszow (Reisha)

Sixteen thousand Jews lived in this eastern Polish town before the war. The Jewish community dates back to the sixteenth century. By the seventeenth century it was a well established community belonging to the "Council of Four Lands" (Vaad Arba Aratzot) with a synagogue and social institutions. Most of the Jews were orthodox, but other movements also existed.

The well-known personalities included Rabbi Aharon Lewin, who was elected to the Polish Sejm (parliament) and literary figures Abba Appelbaum and Itzhak Holzer, and translator Moshe Geszwind. The famous rabbis were Shmuel Halevi, Jacob Reischner and Aaron Lewin. The ghetto

MAP OF RZESZOW

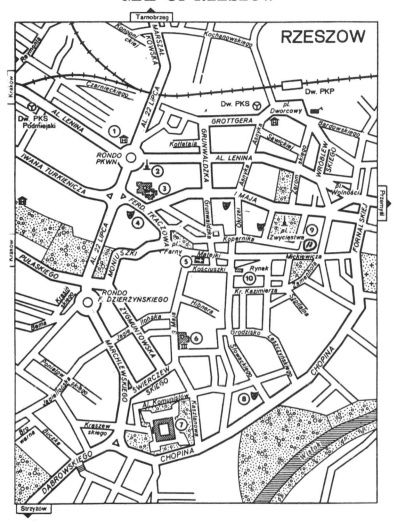

9. Synagoga Nowomiejska (New Town Synagogue)
   is now an art gallery.
11. Synagoga Staromiejska (Old Town Synagogue)

was established in June 1941. By February 1944 no Jews were left. Most of them perished in Belzec and Auschwitz.

After the war 600 Jews returned, but they left after the anti-Semitic disturbances of June 1945.

There are two synagogues at Plac Zwyciestwa (Square): the Old Town Synagogue, called Mala (Small), which was built in the early seventeenth century, and presently houses the archives; and the New Town Synagogue, called Duza (Big), from 1710, presently an art gallery.

A monument at the Jewish cemetery at Ulica Rejtana (the corner of Dolowej) commemorates the Jewish victims of the area. There are about 600 matzevot at cemetery.

Mass Graves: See listing for Glogow Malopolski.

Rzymanow

Jews constituted 40 percent of the town's population. Part of it was expelled by the Germans to Soviet-occupied Poland. In August 1942 all the able-bodied men were deported to labor camp in Plaszow; the remaining to the death camp in Belzec.

A mini museum at Bielackiego 3 displays some Jewish memorabilia.

A ruined synagogue is at Bieleckiego. Cemetery at Slowackiego has some 200 gravestones and monuments honoring the victims of Shoah and the local Tzadikim.

Sanok

By 1570 there were 18 Jewish families in Sanok.

Some famous citizens of Sanok included Benjamin Katz, the head of Tel Aviv University, and Rabbi Meir Shapiro.

Before the outbreak of World War II there were 50 thousand Jews in Sanok. Most of them perished in Belzec.

The synagogue is now a commercial building. Cemetery with 50 graves at Kiczury Street.

Sandomierz (Zuzmir)

There were 40 Jewish families in Sandomierz in 1550. The year 1968 witnessed an accusation for ritual murder against Aaron Berk. By the end of the 1930s the Jewish population constituted 34 percent of the population. Liquidation of the ghetto took place in January of 1943 by deporation to Treblinka.

Synagogue at Basztowa 4 (opposite Urzad Miejski city office) is now the achives of Sandomierz. The cemetery at Basztowa was destroyed. The cemetery at Sucha features a few stones and a memorial.

Sedziszow Malopolski

There is a Jewish cemetery at Ulica (Street) Cicha. A monument at a mass grave with an inscription in Hebrew and Yiddish honors victims of the ghetto that was located here. The inhabitants were deported to Belzec, and 680 people were shot on the spot.

Sewerynowo (Czerwonka Parish)

At Waski Las a tablet marks a place of mass execution of 500 Jews and Poles who suffered from incurable diseases and were shot in the forest on February 12, 1942.

Siedlce (Shedlitz)

The Jewish community dates back to the sixteenth century. Before the war the community was 15 thousand (nearly 50 percent of the population). It had a hospital, Bikur Cholim, Yeshiva and a couple of Yiddish papers. August 1942 witnessed the mass deportation to Treblinka.

A memorial to Jewish victims of the Nazis, in the form of a pyramid of two thousand Jewish tombstones collected from other cemeteries, stands in the local Jewish cemetery where eleven thousand Jews were shot.

Ulica Bohaterow Getta (Heroes of the Ghetto Street) is a stone monument that honors 17 thousand Jews of Siedlce who were deported to Treblinka. Another monument is at Berka Joselewicza.

Siemiatycze (Semyatitcha)

Jews of Siemiatycze were mentioned for the first time in the middle of the sixteenth century. By the nineteenth century 75 percent of the town's population was Jewish, mainly occupied in dealing in grain and timber trades.

On the eve of World War II there were 7000 Jews in town. The ghetto was established in August 1942. It was liquidated in November 1942 by deportation of its inhabitants to Treblinka.

The cemetery at Ulica Kosciuszki was nearly completely destroyed. A plaque at the cemetery commemorates a mass grave of Jews of Siemiatycze. The synagogue at Ulica Swierczewskiego was rebuilt after the war.

Sieradz

The Jews came to Sieradz in the fourteenth century. By 1812 the Jewish quarter existed with its own cemetery. Jews were active in public life of the town and Israel Kempinski became city counselor in 1862.

There were nearly three thousand Jews in Sieradz in 1939. The ghetto was liquated in August 1942. The synagogue at Ulica Wodna 14 is now a cooperative. The cemetery at Ulica Zakladnikow was destroyed.

Sieniawa

Cemetery with 200 gravestones.

Sieroniowice

A symbolic grave marks the location of the forced labor camp.

Skala

There is a mass grave of 1,000 victims at the Jewish cemetery.

Skarczewy

Near Lake Borowno a plaque commemorates a few hundred Jews executed in October and November 1939. The oldest gravestone is from 1873. The area also was a location of a slave labor camp.

Skierniewice (Skiernivitz)

The Jews came to Skierniewice in the nineteenth century and by 1933 over four thousand Jews constituted 33 percent of the population. It was a center of the Chassidic movement led by Tzadik Shimon Kalisz, who established his court in Skierniewice in 1866.

The ghetto was established in 1940 and liquidated by deportation of its population to the Warsaw ghetto.

The cemetery at Ulica Srobowska was destroyed.

The nineteenth-century synagogue at Ulica Batorego 17/19 is being restored to will eventually used as a library.

Slubice

A mass grave and monument honors victims of the German occupation. The cemetery was completely destroyed.

Slupsk

There is a monument at Ulica (Street) Kollataja for the victims of the local concentration camp, which was a branch of the Stutthof concentration camp. The prisoners worked on the railway maintenance (Reichsbahnausbesserer Unswerk). The remaining prisoners lost their lives while being evacuated by sea in April 1945 to Stutthof camp. The cemetery was completely destroyed.

Slutsk

The synagogue is now a bakery.

Sokolow Podlaski

The Jews settled here in the sixteenth century. On the eve of World War II over 50 percent of the population (four thousand people) were Jewish.

The town is known for its Tzadikim Elimelech and Zelig Morgensztern. The mass deportation to Treblinka took place in September 1942.

The synagogue at Ulica Bohaterow Chodakowa 29 was rebuilt after the war and is now a store. The nearby cemetery was destroyed and is now a park.

The synagogue at Ulica Piekna is now stores and apartments. Nearby memorial stone (Piekna) honors 1000 Jews killed on September 3, 1942.

Sobibor

The death camp established here in March 1942 lasted 18 months (until October 1943), and some 250 thousand Jews were murdered. On October 14, 1943, a revolt led by a

PLAN OF THE DEATH CAMP IN SOBIBOR

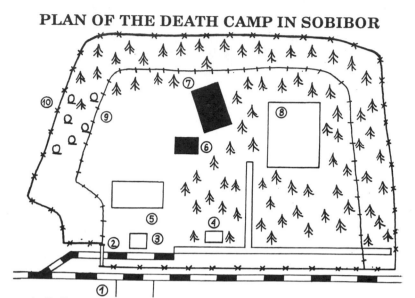

1. Railway station
2. Ramp
3. Shed
4. Pit containing chloride of lime
5. Gas chambers
7. Pits where human remains were buried
8. Kitchens, etc.
9. Barbed wire fence
10. Barbed wire obstacles

Russian officer, Alexander Pieczorski took place. During the revolt some 300 prisoners were able to escape.

Sosnowiec (Sosnovitz)

By the end of ninteenth century nearly 30 percent of the population was Jewish. On the eve of of the war the community was comprised of 28 thousand people with schools, orphanage, hospital, Yeshivot and old age home.

The German army destroyed the synagogue in the first days the occupation. Most of the Jews of Sosnowiec perished in Auschwitz.

There is a Jewish cemetery at Ulica (Street) Gospodarcza. An obelisk honors 20 thousand Jews deported from the area. A total of 24 thousand Sosnowiec Jews were deported to Auschwitz. The bulk of the liquidation took place between August 1-6, 1943, when 10 thousand Sosnowiec Jews were deported. Only a few escaped in bunkers or under Aryan papers. There are about 300 matzevot in the cemetery.

Stawice

A monument marks the place of the mass executions of 300 Jews and Poles in the forest near the road to Nowograd on July 22, 1943.

Stoczek

A memorial tablet at the Jewish cemetery at Ulica Wegrowska honors the Jews of Stoczek. The ghetto was liquidated in the fall of 1942 and its inhabitants deported to Treblinka.

Strachowice

During the war some Jews worked at armament factories. Most perished in Treblinka and Auschwitz.

At Ulica (Street) Dr. Anki, a monument to the Freedom Fighters also honors Jews from the neighboring labor camps shot together with Poles. There is also a cemetery at Podgorze Street with 200 matzevot. A cemetery at Stycznia 17 has 450 matzevot.

Strzyzow

The synagogue is now a commercial building. Cemeteries Ulica Wschodnia, Ulica Przeclawska and Daszynskiego were all destroyed. The local museum at Rynek 28 has some Judaica articles.

Stutthof (Sztutow)

Stutthof was a concentration camp established at the beginning of the German invasion of Poland in 1939. Eighty-five thousand people lost their lives at Stutthof. The camp was liberated by the Red Army on May 9, 1945. A monument designed by Wiktor Tolkin is located on the spot where the Germans burned the bodies of their victims.

MAP OF STUTTHOF CAMP

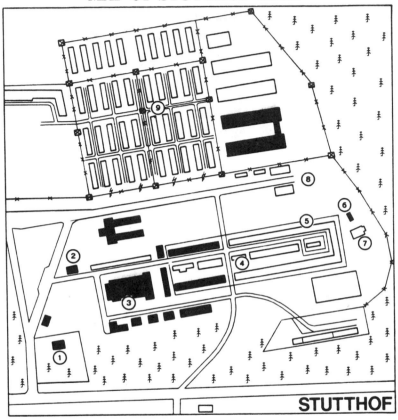

1. Commandant's villa
2. Watch house
3. Commandant's office
4. Prisoners' barracks
5. Hospital
6. Gas chamber
7. Crematorium
8. Monument
9. New camp

Deportation of the Jews from the Baltic Republics to Stutthof Camp

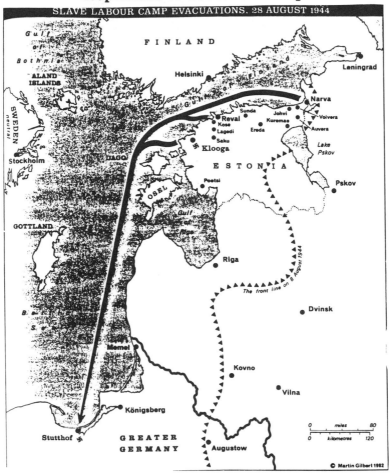

SLAVE LABOUR CAMP EVACUATIONS, 28 AUGUST 1944

COURTESY OF MARTIN GILBERT

Suwalki

There is a cemetery at Engelsa Street. There are only 20 matzevot left. The house of worship is today a municipal libary.

Swarzedz

A tablet at the railway station honors the memory of Jews

who worked on the railway tracks from 1941 to 1943. Some victims were buried in the back of the Catholic cemetery. The cemetery at Poznanska Street was destroyed and is now used as a park.

Swidnica

House of worship is at Bohaterow Getta 22. The cemetery at Szarych Szeregow has a few dozen matzevot.

Szczebrzeszyn

There were three thousand Jews in Szczebrzeszyn. They perished in Belzec. The seventeenth- century synagogue is now a library.

Szczecin (Stetin)

Community and house of worship is at Niemcewicza 2. The cemetery at Ojca Bejzymy Street has a few dozen gravestones remaining.

Szczucin

There is a grave of some Polish soldiers and officers killed by the Germans on September 12, 1939, as well as 20 Jews who were used by the Germans to bury the victims. Cemetery at 1 Maja Street has 50 matzevot. The community (800 people) perished in Belzec.

Szewnia Gora

A monument in the woods near the road from Krasnobor to Zamosc marks the place of execution of Jews, Poles and Soviet partisans.

Szubin

Nowy Swiat, a monument commemorates a so-called "Male Ghetto" (Small Ghetto), which contained about 100 Jews of Nowy Swiat. The cemetery at Keynska Street was destroyed.

Szydlow

North of the market square stands a late-Gothic synagogue from the beginning of the sixteenth century with

MAP OF SZYDLOW

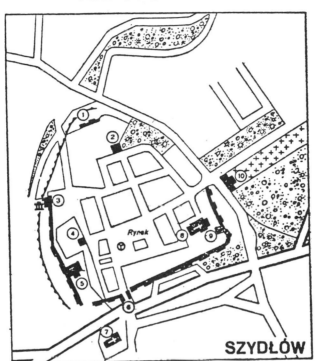

2 - Synagogue

fragments of late-Renaissance interiors. At present it serves as a library.

Szydlowiec

A tablet at the Jewish cemetery honors 16 thousand Jews from the Szydlowiec ghetto. The ghetto at Wschodnia was liquidated on January 13, 1943, by mass deportation to Treblinka.

The sixteenth-century synagogue is now a library; there is also a cemetery with 2500 matzevot.

Szymanowo

A memorial stone at the crossroads of Szymanowo and Sarnowo marks a place of frequent executions of Jews and Poles.

Tarnogrod

There were 2500 Jews in Tarnogrod before the war. They perished in Treblinka. A memorial for victims of the German terror also honors 82 Jews shot by the German gendarmes on September 2, 1942. The 1686 synagogue is used as a warehouse. Cemetery with 1000 matzevot.

Tarnobrzeg

There were 3800 Jews in Tarnobrzeg before the war. The atrocities started on the first day of German occupation. Wehrmacht executed many Jews in the Town Square. The synagogue was rebuilt in the 1970s and is now used as a library. Cemetery at Ulica Sieniewicza was destroyed and is now used as a market place.

Tarnow (Tarna)

Also known as "Tarna," Tarnow is east of Cracow. Before the war 50 percent of the inhabitants were Jewish. The community existed there since the fifteenth century. Tarnow had educational institutions supported by Baron Hirsh as well as many Zionist organizations, including Agudat Hashachar, Ahavat Zion, Hamizrahi, Hovevei Zion, Hechalutz, Revisionists, Bnei Akiva, and Bund.

The Tarnow ghetto was liquidated on February 9, 1944, when the remaining 150 Jews were sent to Plaszow the camp. After the war 700 Jews came back to Tarnow. By 1965 only 65 remained.

The old cemetery at Ulica (Street) Nowodebrowska includes mass graves of 15 thousand Jews murdered during the German occupation.

The Jewish cemetery here has a memorial to Nazi victims. A credit union (Towrzystwo Kredytowe) is at Ulica Goldhammera 5, where tablets commemorate Herman Marz, president of the Jewish community, and Eliasz Goldhamer, deputy-mayor.

Old age home (Dom Starcow) is at Nowodebrowska 25; all its occupants were murdered by the Germans.

Yavneh high school is at Ulica Baluta 6. Orphanage at Ulica Kollataja 14 is presently a kindergartern. School and library at Ulica Sw. Anny 1. Local museum at the Rynek (City Square) has some Judaica items.

Plac Bohaterow Ghetta honors heroes of the Ghetto Square at Ulica Zydowska, the Jewish street.

A solitary pillar, remnant of the synagogue still stands and will be permanently preserved by incorporation into a new building to be erected on the site.

A monument at the Jewish cemetery at Ulica (Street) Szpitalna honors 20 thousand Jews of Tarnow killed by the Germans.

Tomaszow Lubelski

Jews came to Tomaszow in the early seventeeth century. There were 6000 Jews before World War II. The community had sports clubs and a library. The famous rabbis of the town were Itzhak Shapira and Yehuda Ben Nissan Meir.

The obelisk at Ulica (Street) Kosciuszki honors executed inhabitants of the town at the time of the liquidation of the ghetto.

Tomaszow Mazawiecki

Jews came to Tomaszow in the beginning of nineteenth century on the inviation of Count Antoni Ostrowski. They established a textile industry and eventually the community had a synagogue, Bet Hamidrash, financial institutions and high school.

By 1939 there were 13 thousand Jews in Tomaszow. The Germans burned the synagogue in 1939, but some Sifrei Torah were hidden and were recovered after the war. The ghetto was established in December 1941 and liquated in 1942 by mass deportations to camps.

Cemetery at Ulica Smutna 19 was established in 1831 on the grounds donated by Count Ostrowski. It has a wall around it and features 2000 matzevot.

Torun

There were about 1000 Jews in Torun on the eve of World

War II. The community had a synagogue and educational system of its own, as well as other social institutions.

There is a mass grave of the 152 Jewish women from the Charabio work camp killed by the Germans before the evacuation of the camp on January 18. The cemetery was destroyed.

Trawniki

Trawniki was the site of a concentration camp, originally set up as a POW camp for Soviet prisoners in June 1941. In the fall of 1942 it was converted into a work camp for Jews from Poland, Austria, Germany, Czechoslovakia, Belgium, Holland and France. On November 3, 1943, the remaining 10 thousand prisoners were murdered. A monument marks the site. (See Poniatowo)

Treblinka

Treblinka I was a forced labor camp created in 1941 and liquidated in July 1944. During its existence some 20 thousand victims passed through its gates.

Treblinka II was a death camp created in the spring of 1942. A make-believe railway station was built by the Nazis and camouflaged as a small rural station. Timetables and advertisements were posted on the walls to disguise the real purpose. From across the continent of Europe freight trains came to deposit victims at this railway station. The camp operated 13 gas chambers. On August 2, 1943, an armed revolt of the prisoners took place. A few prisoners managed to escape. In the 13 months (July 1942 to August 1943) the camp existed, 874,600 people, mainly from Warsaw, perished.

A symbolic cemetery for about 750 thousand to 900 thousand Jews from Central Poland, Germany, Austria, Czechoslovakia, France, the Netherlands, Belgium, the USSR, Yugoslavia and other countries is on the site of the former center of immediate extermination in Treblinka. The monument there consists of some 17 thousand stones marked with names of the cities and countries from which the Jews came. There is a map at the entrance to the camp showing the location of stones commemorating people from specific communities. There is a stone devoted to one person Janusz Korczak (Heryk Goldszmit) and his children. The central part of the monument is in the form of a menorah with the inscription "Never Again" in a number of languages, including Yiddish.

Trzebinia (Chebin)

An obelisk at Kruczkowskiewgo (opposite the refinery) honors Jewish victims of the labor camp, which existed there in the years 1942 to 1945. Cemetery at Ulica Slowackiego has 200 matzevot in various stages of destruction.

Turek

A monument at Ulica (Street) Kolska commemorates victims of executions that took place at the market place in the fall of 1939-1940.

The synagogue is now a cooperative. The cemetery is destroyed.

Monument in Turek

Tykocin (Tiktin)

Also known as Tiktin, this is a small town near Bialystok.

The Jewish community was established in 1552, and consisted of 2,500 on the eve of World War II (in effect the majority of the inhabitants). It had a "Tarbut" school and Zionist organization.

The memorial at Lopuchowo commemorates 1,600 Jews of Tykocin murdered by "Kommando Bialystok," led by Warsaw Gestapo man Wolfgang Birkner.

An early baroque house of prayer from 1642 was made of brick in the form of a fortress, and is located at Kozia. Beautifully restored, it is a typical example of Jewish architecture and now serves as a Jewish museum. Well worth the trip, a stop at Tykocin could be combined with a visit to Treblinka or Bialystok. Cemetery established in 1522 features 500 matzevot.

Tyszowce

A tablet at the offices of the parish building honors 1,000 Jews shot by the German gendarmes on June 16, 1942. Cemetery destroyed. Presently there is a pre-school building in the old area.

Ustszyki-Dolne

The synagogue is now a library. The cemetery has 80 gravestones.

Uzarzewo

A tablet on the mass grave commemorates Jews murdered in the labor camps of Groszczyna and Kobylnica.

Walbzych

Community and house of worship located at Mickiewicza 18.

Warsaw (Warszawa)

First mention of Jewish presence in Warsaw goes back to 1414. Famous rabbis of Warsaw were Solomon Zalman Lipszyc, Dov-Ber Meisels, Yaakov Gesundheit and Chaim Davidson.

All political parties were represented here. A number of newspapers were published in Warsaw even during the occupation, such as underground *Davar* and *El Al*.

WARSAW AREA

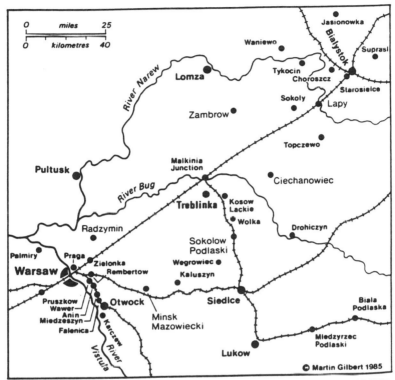

COURTESY OF MARTIN GILBERT

The 390 thousand Jews who lived in Warsaw toward the end of 1939 made up one-third of the city's total population (November 30, 1939, census showed 359,827). The Jewish intelligentsia, industrialists and merchants, craftsmen and workers had lived there for generations. The political, social and cultural life of the Polish Jews, and indeed European Jewry, was focused there.

Jewish Community Headquarters, 6 Twarda (Street), is located in a compound of sorts, which includes a kosher kitchen, a mikvah, a synagogue, a theater and a cultural association. This is also the national headquarters of the Union of Jewish Religious Communities (Zwiazek Regligijny Wyznania Mojzeszowego). All of the social work here is supported by the American Joint Distribution Committee (Joint).

Jewish Cultural House, 3 Plac (Pl.) Grzybowski, was opened in 1966. The building (near the synagogue) houses the Jewish Cultural-Social Association (Towarzystwo Kulturalne Zydow w Polsce) and the **Yiddish State Theater** of Poland (moved from Lodz). The theater was made famous by its star performer and director, Ida Kaminska (who moved to New York in 1968). She was the daughter of Esther, the mother of the Jewish theater after whom the theater was named.

The Jewish theater was revived right after the liberation of Lublin. It moved to Wroclaw in 1949 and joined a considerable Jewish population in that city at that time. Two years later another theater opened in Lodz. The two theaters were united in 1950 as the State Jewish Theater, named after Esther R. Kaminski. In 1955 it moved to Warsaw. Personalities such as Abraham Morewski, Ida Kaminski, Chewel Buzgan, Juliusz Berger, Mieczylaw Bram, Adam Czarka, Seweryn Dalecki, Piotr Erlich, Estera Kowalska, Herman Lercher, Jakub Rotbaum, Szymon Szurmiej, Michal Szweklich, and Tywa Szyler-Buzgan became famous throughout the Jewish theatrical world. Since 1970 the theater has been under the management of Szymon Szurmiej, the leading actor of the theater and a former member of the Sejm (Parliament).

The same building also houses the editorial offices of the a Yiddish publishing house for the *Folks-Sztym*, Poland's only Jewish newspaper published in Yiddish and Polish. Jewish cooperatives are also located in this building.

Nozyk Synagogue of Warsaw at 6 Twarda is part of the Jewish community compound. It was founded in 1902 by a Warsaw merchant, Zalman Nozyk, at a cost of 250 thousand roubles. The building, which was nearly destroyed by the Germans, was rebuilt after the war and reconstructed in recent years. It is the only synagogue presently in existence in Warsaw. The great synagogue at Tlomackie designed by Leandro Marconi in 1887 was blown up by the Nazis after the Warsaw ghetto uprising. It was located next to the present building of the Jewish Historical Institute.

The Nozyk synagogue was only one among the many houses of prayer in Warsaw that survived World War II. The synagogue has even witnessed recently a few bar mitzvah ceremonies, among them one of Daniel Palzur, son recent Israeli ambassador. Before the war Warsaw had several hundred houses of prayer, the major ones situated at 4 Twarda Street (named for P. Serdyner), 20 Wspolna Street (named for M.A. Kustman), 5 Gesia Street (named for M. Bruner), 49 Okopowa Street, and 8 Brodnowska Street. Among the synagogues destroyed were Zionist ones including Ohel Moshe and Moriah.

On the other hand, there were only three synagogues in Warsaw that had been specifically designed as synagogues with the distinctive architectural form. The oldest one, situated on the corner of Szeroka and Petersburska streets (today Wojcika and Jagielonska), was built in 1840 to Jozef Lessel's design. It survived until 1939. Devastated during the war, it was to be reconstructed, but it was too thoughtlessly and hastily demolished.

The most famous synagogue, called the Great Synagogue on Tlomackie, was designed by Leandro Marconi. Its construction took several years and the ceremony of inauguration was held in 1878. It was not Hasidic in design, but very similar to the Oranienburgerstrasse synagogue in Berlin and also to St. Charles Borromeo Church in Vienna and the

Model of Great Synagogue in Warsaw

Palace of Justice in Brussels. It provided seating for 1,100, and it served the more assimilated inhabitants of Warsaw. (In fact the synagogue's Rabbi Samuel Poznanski translated the prayerbook into Polish.) It was blown up by Nazi troops under the command of General Stroop on May 16, 1943, following the uprising in the Warsaw ghetto. A detailed model of Tlomackie synagogue recently has been put on display at Beth Hatefutzot (Diaspora Museum) in Tel Aviv.

The only synagogue of the three that has survived until our times is one synagogue named after Rywka and Zalman Nozyk. The merchant Zalman Nozyk, Manasse's son, bought the site for the construction of the future synagogue in 1893. Five years later in the spring of 1898, the construction of the synagogue began and took four years; the cost of construction, very high for that time, was covered by Zalman Nozyk from his own funds.

The religious opening of the synagogue took place on May 12, 1902, on Lag ba-Omer. Apart from the founder, the committee of the newly built synagogue included I. Ettinger, D.M. Szereszewski, L.I. Dawidsohn, and Z. Krakow. Owing to the similarity of architectural layout between the Nozyk synagogue and the Great Synagogue at Tlomacka, it is speculated that it could also have been designed by Leandro Marconi, though tradition gives another name, namely that of the architect Prechner. The Nozyk synagogue was built in the Neo-Romanesque style with Neo-Byzantine stucco ornaments, as a manifestation of the electic tendencies of that time.

During the occupation, the synagogue was used by the Nazis for a stable and fodder storage, thus causing considerable devastation. Bombardments of the city during the Warsaw uprising in 1944 caused much damage to the roof and part of the elevation. After the war (in the late 1940s), it was roughly reconstructed and put to religious use. The thorough reconstruction under supervision of architects Hanna Szczepanowska and Eva Dziedzic took place from 1977 to 1983. During the reconstruction new quarters for the Religious Union of the Mosaic Faith in the Polish People's Republic were added at the eastern wall. The official opening took place on April 18, 1983.

After years of absence, a rabbi now officiates at the Nozyk synagogue. Rabbi Menachem Joskowitz, an Israeli import, arrived in Warsaw in 1989. His presence in Poland has been supported by the Lauder Foundation. The synagogue has been seeing a renaissance with large attendances at monthly concerts of recorded *hazzanut,* the songs of the famed cantors. Rabbi Besser, who heads the Lauder Foundation and visits Poland regularly, says that as many as 300 people now attend Shabbat services in the synagogue, and that at least 700 people attend the concerts.

As a historical monument, the synagogue is open to the public on Thursdays from 10 a.m. to 3 p.m.

Warsaw Ghetto Area (See map on next page)

From the middle of 1940, the Warsaw Jews and those deported from other towns as well as those brought in from the Western European countries, were enclosed within the ghetto walls. The population of the Warsaw ghetto grew to nearly 500 thousand people, all living in terrifying conditions and suffering from starvation and disease. In the summer of 1942, mass deportations to the death camps, predominantly Treblinka, began. In January 1943, when the ghetto still contained 60 thousand people, the first Jewish military resistance action was organized, forcing the Nazis to retreat and temporarily abandon their ultimate goal: the total destruction of the ghetto. On April 19, of the same year, an uprising broke out within the ghetto walls. The fighters of the Jewish Combat Organization (Z.O.B.), led by Mordechai Anielewicz, together with those of the Jewish Military Union (Z.Z.W), led by Mordechai Tenenbaum, numbered several hundred people and used a well-constructed network of bunkers and defenses. They were attacked by over two thousand heavily armed Wehrmacht soldiers and SS troops. After a ferocious struggle on May 8, the main bunker at 18 Mila Street fell, burying the staff of the Jewish Combat Organization and its commander Anielewicz. On May 16, to celebrate their victory, the Nazis blew up the nearby Great Synagogue in Tlomackie. In

MAP OF WARSAW GHETTO

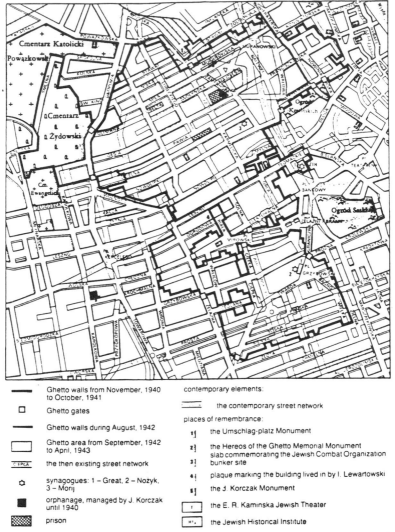

▬	Ghetto walls from November, 1940 to October, 1941	contemporary elements:
□	Ghetto gates	═══ the contemporary street network
▬	Ghetto walls during August, 1942	places of remembrance:
▭	Ghetto area from September, 1942 to April, 1943	1] the Umschlag-platz Monument
⌐EPCA	the then existing street network	2] the Hereos of the Ghetto Memorial Monument slab commemorating the Jewish Combat Organization
✿	synagogues: 1 – Great, 2 – Nożyk, 3 – Morij	3] bunker site
■	orphanage, managed by J. Korczak until 1940	4] plaque marking the building lived in by I. Lewartowski
▨	prison	5] the J. Korczak Monument
		the E. R. Kaminska Jewish Theater
		the Jewish Historical Institute

COURTESY OF ORBIS

some places in the ghetto fighting continued until July. Some of those who survived managed to escape through the sewers to the Aryan side. In his report to headquarters, the Nazi commander Juergen Stroop gave the figures of 56,065

Jews captured, 7,000 exterminated and 5,565 killed in action. The Polish underground press evaluated the enemy's losses at 400 killed and about 1,000 wounded. The uprising in the Warsaw ghetto triggered similar actions, but on a smaller scale, in the ghettos in Bialystok, Czestochowa, Bedzin and Cracow.

Warsaw Ghetto Uprising Monument, Anielewicza and Zamenhof streets, commemorates the revolt of the Jews in the Warsaw ghetto against the Nazi occupation forces, and stands on the site of the Central Command Post where the first shots were fired at dawn on April 19, 1943. Designed by Natan Rapaport, the 36-foot monument is a bronze statue group mounted in front of a towering granite wall. The granite originally had been ordered from Sweden by Hitler's sculptor Arno Breker for a projected victory monument. The inscription, in Yiddish, Hebrew and Polish, reads, "The Jewish People-To Its Heroes, and Its Martyrs." A sister monument is located at Yad Vashem in Jerusalem and was unveiled on the 5th anniversary.

A circular memorial marks the manhole cover exit from the sewer used by the ghetto fighters. This was the first memorial plaque erected on the fifth anniversary of the Warsaw ghetto uprising. On the forty-fifth anniversary a series of stone markers were constructed along the path from the Warsaw ghetto uprising monument to Zygelbojm Square, Mila 18 and Umschlagplatz (along Zamenhoff and Stawki streets). They describe, in Polish and Hebrew, various facets of the martyrdom and fight of the Warsaw Jews. The markers, called "Memory Lane," were designed by architects Z. Gasior and S. Jankowski. Signs in the memory lane honor individuals and commemorate events in the life of the Warsaw ghetto:

1. Memory Tree
2. Creation of the Ghetto in 1940
3. Ghetto uprising April 19 to
4. May 15, 1943
5. Emmanual Ringelblum
6. Jozef Lewartowski, Socialist party activist executed in 1942 (posthumously awarded Grunwald Cross)

7. Michal Klepfisz, Bund activist killed in action on the second day of the uprising (posthumously awarded order Virtuti Militari)
8. Shumuel Zygelbojm
9. Shumuel Zygelbojm, also
10. Arieh Wilner, "Jurek," Hashomer Hatzair activist and liaison officer between the Jewish and Polish undergrounds. Perished with the command of the uprising on May 8, 1943. (Posthumously awarded order Virtuti Militari).
11. Mordechai Anielewicz, member of Hashomer Hatzair and commander of Z.O.B.—Jewish Combat Organizaiton and the leader of the uprising committed suicide with the rest of his command on May 8, 1943 at Mila 18 (posthumously awarded Grunwald Cross).
12. Meir Majerowicz,"Marek," member of Poalei Zion (posthumously awarded Cross of Valor).
13. Frumka Plotnicka, liasion officer between Jewish underground units in Warsaw, Sosnowiec and Bedzin, killed in action (posthumously awarded Grunwald Cross).
14. Rabbi Itzhak Nyssenbaum, leader of religious Zionists and member of the ghetto underground organization, perished in Treblinka.
15. Janusz Korczak (Henryk Goldszmidt), educator, physician and writer perished with the children of his orphanage whom he refused to abandon.
16. Ichak (Itzhak) Katzenelson, Hebrew and Yiddish poet, author of *The Song about the Murdered Jewish Nation*," perished in Auschwitz.
17. At Stawki 5/7 in this building was located the SS command of the Umshlagplatz, which oversaw the deporation of thousands of inhabitants of the ghetto to Trelinka.
18. At Stawki 6/8 in this building of the school and temporary hospital Jews were held before deporation to Treblinka.

The bunker where Anielewicz and his commanders met their deaths was in the building at **18 Mila (Mila 2/4)**

Street, where there is a small memorial in the form of a mound and a monument. The inscription reads: "On this spot on May 8, 1943, Mordechai Anielewicz, commander of the Warsaw Uprising, met Solider's Death together with the rest of the command of the Jewish Combat Organization in their struggle against German occupiers. Between the Mila 18 and the Ghetto Memorial, is a small square named after Szmuel Zygelbojm, member of the Polish National Council in London, who at the end of the uprising committed suicide in protest of the world's indifference. On the house next to the notorious **Umschlagplatz**, where the Nazis carried out their "selections" for deportation, three simple plaques inscribed in Polish, Hebrew and Yiddish, affixed to the wall on Stawki Street, tell the tragic story. A full-scale memorial is to be erected on the present site of the gas station, which will be removed. The first phase of the memorial (designed by Hanna Szmalenberg and Wladyslaw Klamerus) was completed in April 1988 to coincide with the forty-fifth anniversary of the ghetto uprising. The inscription reads: "Along this path of suffering and death over 300,000 were driven in 1942/1943 from the Warsaw Ghetto to the gas chambers of the Nazi extermination camps." First names of Polish Jews are engraved on the walls of the monument in a fashion similar to the Vietnam War Memorial in Washington.

Ulica (Street) Anielewicza is named for Mordechai Anielewicz, commander of the Jewish Combat Organization (Z.O.B) in the heroic revolt of the Jews of the Warsaw ghetto in 1943. He was barely 20 when he was arrested by the Soviet authorities in 1939 for organizing the emigration of Jews from the Russian-occupied areas of Poland to Palestine. Released in 1940, he became the leader of Jewish underground groups in Vilna and Czestochowa until his appointment in 1942 as commander-in-chief of the Jewish Combat Organization. He and the members of his command committed suicide rather than fall into German hands. It was the most heroic struggle of the Jewish people against the Nazis. It was unique among all the underground battles; from the military point of view, it lacked all of the three basic prerequisites for a successful uprising, i.e., a choice of time, place and hope.

Mordechai Anielewicz's Last Letter

The last wish of my life has been fulfilled.

It is now clear to me that what took place exceeded all expectations. In our opposition to the Germans we did more than our strength allowed but now our forces are waning. We are on the brink of extinction. We forced the Germans to retreat twice but they returned stronger than before.

One of our group held out for forty minutes; and another fought for about six hours. The mine which was laid in the area of the brush factory exploded as planned. Then we attacked the Germans and they suffered heavy casualties. Our losses were generally low. That is an accomplishment too. Z. fell, next to his machine gun.

I feel that great things are happening and that this action which we have dared to take is of enormous value.

We have no choice but to go over to partisan methods of fighting as of today. Tonight, six fighting groups are going out. They have two tasks to reconnoiter the area and to capture weapons. Remember, short range weapons are of no use to us. We employ them very rarely. We need many rifles, hand grenades, machine guns and explosives.

I cannot describe the conditions in which the Jews of the ghetto are now "living." Only a few exceptional individuals will be able to survive such suffering. The others will sooner or later die. Their fate is certain, even though thousands are trying to hide in cracks and rat holes. It is impossible to light a candle, for lack of air. Greetings to you who are outside. Perhaps a miracle will occur and we shall see each other again one of these days. It is extremely doubtful.

The last wish of my life has been fulfilled. Jewish self-defense has become a fact. Jewish resistance and revenge have become actualities. I am happy to have been one for the first Jewish fighters in the ghetto.

> Where will rescue come from?
> Mordechai Anielewicz
> During the revolt, Warsaw 1943.

Ulica (Street) Fundamanskiego, was named for

Ephraim Fundamanski, one of the organizers of the Warsaw gbetto uprising.

Ulica Lewartowska (Street), between Gesia and Anielewicz St. (Ulica), memorializes Joseph Lewartowski, one of the leaders of the ghetto underground.

Ulica Pereca (Street), the former Ceglana (Street), is named for Isaac Loeb Perec, who lived and worked in Warsaw from 1887 until his death in 1915. His stories and poems in Yiddish describe the hardships of Jewish life in the Eastern European shtetl.

Szterna (Street) Ulica was named for Abraham Sztern, a pioneer of the Haskalah movement in Poland, director of the rabbinical seminary, and inventor of an early 19th century adding machine.

Some other streets were named after Jews including one of the main avenues of Warsaw, Aleje Jerozolimskie, which at one time led to a Jewish village called "New Jerusalem."

Skwer (Square) Zygelbojma is a small square located between the Ghetto Memorial and Mila 18 and was named after Szmuel Zygelbojm, member of the Polish National Council (Parliament-in-Exile) in London, at the end of the Warsaw ghetto uprising he committed suicide to protest the world's indifference.

I Cannot Keep Silent and
Cannot Continue to Live

Mr. President, Mr. Premier,

I take the liberty to address my last words to you and through your intermediary to the Polish government and Polish people, to the governments and peoples of the Allied nations, to the conscience of the world.... .

I cannot keep silent and cannot continue to live when the remnants of the Jewish people in Poland, whom I represent, are perishing.

Our comrades in the Warsaw Ghetto lost their lives, fighting with arms in hand, in a last heroic rising. I was not given the opportunity to perish as they did, together with them. But I belong to them, and should share their mass grave.

My death is to serve as the deepest protest against the passivity with which the world looks at all this and permits the annihilation of the Jewish people. I know how little human life means, especially today. But since I was unable to achieve it during my lifetime, perhaps my death will help to shatter the indifference of those who could and should do something about it, so that now, at the very last moment, that handful of Polish Jews who are still alive could be saved from extermination.

My life belongs to the Jewish people in Poland, that is why I sacrifice it. It is my desire that this handful which remained of the several-million strong Polish Jewry, could together with the Polish masses look forward to liberation, could breathe the air of freedom and justice of socialism in Poland and the world for all the inhuman torments they suffered. And I believe that precisely such a Poland and such a world will arise...

(Excerpts from the letter and testament addressed to Wladyslaw Raczkiewicz, President of the Polish Republic, and General Wladyslaw Sikorski, premier of the government-in-exile of the Polish Republic, which had its headquarters in London. Szmuel Zygelbojm was, on behalf of the Bund, a member of the National Council, a Polish parliament-in-exile).

National Archeological Museum, 53 Dluga. A collection of Judaica, paintings, and engravings with Jewish themes can be seen at the paintings department.

CHRONOLOGY OF THE WARSAW GHETTO

Events Outside Warsaw   Events in Warsaw

1938
Aug. 21   Germany and
     the Soviet
     Union sign
     nonaggression
     pact, giving
     Germany a free
     hand to invade
     Poland.

Auschwitz memorial at Birkenau

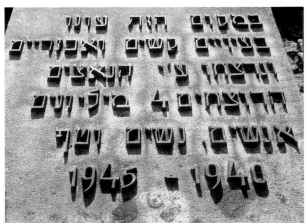

Hebrew inscriptions at Birkenau

BELOW: *Belzec monument designed by M. Welter*

Monument at Bielzyce funded by N. Ariav

Tablet at the Chelmno monument

Chelmno monument designed by J. Stasinski and J. Buszkiewicz

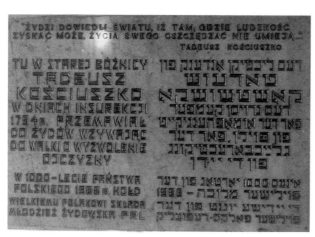

Kosciuszko plaque at the Old Synagogue in Cracow

Marker at Jewish Culture Institute

Plaszow Camp memorial designed by R. Szczypczynski and W. Ceckiewicz

BELOW:
Crawcow Philharmonic Courtesy UJA Archives

Tablet commemorating the Jews of the Lodz ghetto

PAMIĘCI 210 000 ŻYDÓW I CYGANÓW
OFIAR ZBRODNI HITLEROWSKICH

W DNIU 8 II 1940 OKUPACYJNE WŁADZE
HITLEROWSKIE UTWORZYŁY W ŁODZI
W CZĘŚCI BAŁUT I STAREGO MIASTA
GETTO DLA LUDNOŚCI ŻYDOWSKIEJ.
ZAMKNIĘTO W NIM OKOŁO 205 000
ŻYDÓW Z POLSKI CZECHOSŁOWACJI
AUSTRII, LUKSEMBURGA, I NIEMIEC.
W TYM CO NAJMNIEJ 160 000 MIESZKAŃ-
-CÓW ŁODZI. W WYDZIELONYM OBOZIE
OSADZONO PONAD 5000 CYGANÓW
Z AUSTRII I KRAJÓW BAŁKAŃSKICH
W WYNIKU EKSTERMINACYJNEJ
POLITYKI OKUPANTA ZGINĘŁO W
GETCIE I W OBOZIE DLA CYGANÓW
OKOŁO 45 000 OSÓB PONAD 75 000
ZAMORDOWANO W OBOZIE ZAGŁADY
W CHEŁMNIE NAD NEREM.
POZOSTAŁYCH WYWIEZIONO DO RÓŻ-
-NYCH HITLEROWSKICH MIEJSC ZAG-
-ŁADY I ODOSOBNIENIA GŁÓWNIE
DO OŚWIĘCIMIA
PRZEŻYLI NIELICZNI

SPOŁECZEŃSTWO ŁODZI

Kupat Cholim in Lodz

Cemetery gate at Lodz

Mausoleum of the Pozanski family at Lodz cemetery

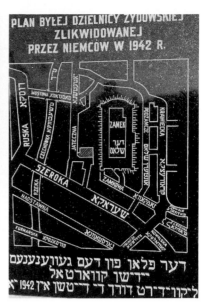

Marker for the location of the Muharshal and Maharam synagogue in Lublin

Plaque on steps of Lublin castle showing old Jewish quarter

Yeshivat Hachamei in Lublin Courtesy UJA Archives

Marker in Old Cemetery of Lublin

Memorial to the Jews of Lublin

Author with grandfather who perished in Majdanek, Lublin 1942

Mausoleum portion of Majdanek monument

Symbolic grave of author's family members who perished in the Holocaust

Majdanek monument designed by W. Tolkin and J. Dembek

Unveiling of monument for Jews of Pulawy Courtesy R. Hoenigsfeld-Calandre

Sobibor monument designed by M. Welter

Entrance to Sobibor camp

Stone commemorating J. Korczak and the children at Treblinka

Mila 18 monument

Symbolic graves for lost communities at Treblinka

Monument of the Heroes of Warsaw ghetto by N. Rapaport
Courtesy of D. Goldberg

ABOVE: *Detail from Warsaw uprising memorial*

LEFT: *Symbolic grave of J. Korczak at Warsaw cemetery*

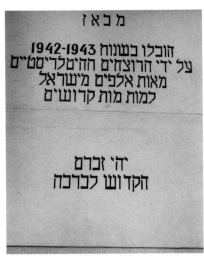

Tablet at Unschlagplatz in Warsaw

Plaque on Memory Lane at Jewish Hospital

Fragment of new Unschlagplatz monument

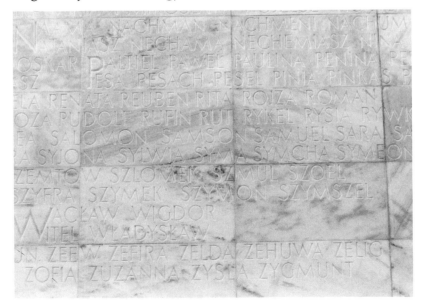

LEFT:
Plaque honoring victims of the Gestapo in Warsaw ghetto

BELOW:
Shumuel Zygelbojm Square in Warsaw

RIGHT:
*J. Korczak
orphanage*

BELOW:
*Statue at
orphanage*

LEFT: *Tomb of Unknown Soldier lists Warsaw ghetto uprising*

BELOW: *Manhole cover that is part of Warsaw ghetto monument*

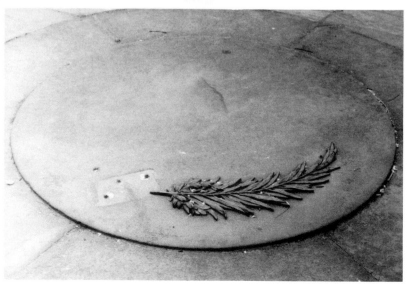

Events Outside Warsaw

Events in Warsaw

1939

Sept. 1 Germany invades Poland. S.S. and Wehrmacht instigate numerous pogroms in Poland.

Sept. 17 Russians invade and occupy Eastern Poland.

Sept. 21 Reinhardt Heydrich, chief of German Security Police, plans ghettos in Poland.

Sept. 27 Warsaw surrenders

Sept. Germany and the Soviet Union partition Poland into three parts: one incorporated into the German Reich, one to the Soviet Union, and one unincorporated, under German protectorate (Government General).

Events Outside Warsaw

Events in Warsaw

Oct. 4   Adam Czerniakow ordered by Gestapo to set up Jewish Council to replace Jewish Community Council within 24 hours.

Oct. 6 Hitler announces his resettlement policy for Poland, including Jewish seclusion.

Oct. 8 Decree reincorporating provinces lost to Poland in 1918 into German Reich; also province of Lodz.

Oct. 12 First deportation of Jews from Vienna and Bohemia to Nisko in Poland.

Oct. 26 Forced labor extended to all Jews living in Government General.

Events Outside Warsaw

Events in Warsaw

Oct. 28   Jewish badge
imposed at
Wloclawek.

Nov.   Census shows
359,827 Jews
in Warsaw.

Nov. 8   Hans Frank
made Governor
General of
Poland.
Attempt to
assassinate
Hitler in
Munich.
Nov. 15   Germans
forced to
readmit Jews
expelled across
Russian lines.
Nov. 23   Jewish badge
made
compulsory
throughout
Government
General.
Nov. 30   Russia attacks
Finland.
1940

Jan. 21 Gestapo orders
registration of
Jewish
property.

Events Outside Warsaw

Events in Warsaw

Jan. 26 Congregational worship forbidden; ritual slaughter prohibited.

March 12 Russia makes peace with Finland.

April 9 Germany invades Denmark and Norway.

April 14 Frank declares that Cracow will be "free of Jews."

April 30 First enclosed and guarded Ghetto set up in Lodz.

May 10 Germans invade Western countries.

May 15 Holland surrenders.

May 28 British evacuate Dunkirk.

June Jewish Council reorganized; limited to carrying out orders of German authorities.

Events Outside Warsaw	Events in Warsaw
June First issue of Jewish newspaper.	
June 10 Italy enters the war.	
June 20 Hitler mentions to Mussolini plan to resettle European Jewry on French island of Madagascar.	
June 21 France signs armistice with Germany.	
July 12 Frank says he has persuaded Hitler to stop deporting Jews to the Government General.	
July 19 Hitler addresses Reichstag, offers peace to Great Britain.	
	Sept. Quarantine area, later to be a ghetto, contains 240 thousand Jews, 80 thousand Christians.

Events Outside Warsaw

Oct. 4   Vichy Jewish
Statute deprives
refugee Jews of
their civil
rights.
Oct. 5   German troops
arrive in
Romania.

Events in Warsaw

Oct. 16   Decree gives
Christians two
weeks to move
out of
quarantine
area and Jews
to move in.
Nov. 15 Warsaw
ghetto sealed
off.

1941

Jan. 11 Frank obtains
postponement of
plans for
deportation of
all Jews to
Government
General.
Jan. 22-23   Iron Guard
revolt in
Romania. First
Jewish
massacre of
war.
Jan. 31 First attempt at
creating a
Jewish Council
in France.

Events Outside Warsaw

Events in Warsaw

Jan.   Jewish Council
census shows
378,979 Jews
in ghetto.

Feb.- Apr. 72 Thousand
Jews deported
to the Warsaw
ghetto.

Jews Expelled into the Warsaw Ghetto

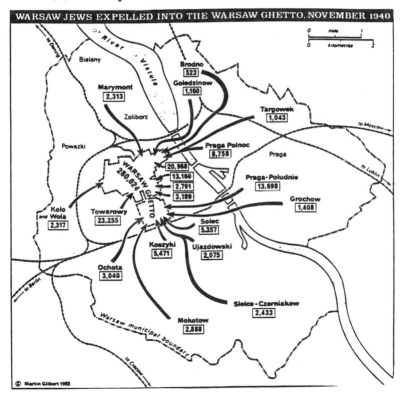

WARSAW JEWS EXPELLED INTO THE WARSAW GHETTO, NOVEMBER 1940

COURTESY OF MARTIN GILBERT

Events Outside Warsaw

Feb. 17 Romania enters
the war.

Events in Warsaw

Feb. 18 Jewish Council
is allowed to
raise a loan
from German
banks on the
security of
blocked Jewish
accounts.

Feb. 22-23 Deportation
of Jewish
hostages from
Amsterdam.

March 1 Bulgaria enters
the war.

March 2 Hitler
outlines plans
for occupation of
Russia.

March 4 Construction
of Bunawerk
factory at
Oswiecim
authorized.

March 30 Vichy
Government
appoints a
Commission on
Jewish
Questions.
British troops in
Greece.

April 6 Germans invade
Yugoslavia and
Greece.

Events Outside Warsaw

Events in Warsaw

April — Schools licensed for 5 thousand of the 50 thousand children in the ghetto. American Joint Distribution Committee allowed to have offices in the ghetto.

May — Census shows 430 thousand Jews in the ghetto.

May 14 Germans intern 3,600 naturalized Parisian Jews.

May 15 Petain broadcasts pledge of cooperation with Germany.

End of May - Einsatzgruppen (special extermination squads) formed.

June 22 Germany invades Russia.

June 25 Romanian pogram at Jassy. (Iassi)

Events Outside Warsaw	Events in Warsaw
June 28 German-inspired pogrom at Kovno, Lithuania.	
	July 17,800 refugees, including 3,300 children, classified as destitute.
	Aug. Three thousand Jews employed in cooperative workshops.
Mid-Aug. Slovak Government disperses Bratislava ghetto.	
	Sept. Frank announces a reduction in ghetto rations. Ghetto post office forbidden to handle foreign mail. End of parcels from neutral countries.
Sept. 1 Massacre of Jews expelled by Hungary, at Kamenets-Podolski.	

Events Outside Warsaw	Events in Warsaw
Sept. 15 Slovakia adopts Nuremberg laws. Jewish badge decreed throughout Greater Reich.	
Sept. 19 Liquidation of Zhitomir ghetto in Ukraine. Germans occupy Kiev.	
Sept. 23 Experimental gassing at Oswiecim.	
Sept. 28-29 Massacre of 34,000 Jews from Kiev.	
Oct. 2 Paris synagogues blown up by secret action of Gestapo.	
	Oct. 5 Death edict for leaving ghetto without permission.
Oct. 12 Moscow partly evacuated.	
Oct. 20 First deportation from Reich decreed (to Lodz).	
	Oct. 23 Liquidation of the small ghetto.

Events Outside Warsaw	Events in Warsaw
Oct. Vast massacres at Riga, Vilna, Kovno, and Dvinsk.	
	Oct. Streetcar lines abolished.
Nov. 4 Lodz deportations completed.	
Nov. 6 Fifteen thousand massacred at Rovno. First Reich Jews arrive in Riga, Minsk, and Kovno.	
End Nov. First massacre at Rostov. Threat to Moscow over.	
	Dec. 1 Receipt of food packages forbidden under pretext of danger of epidemics.
Dec. 7 Pearl Harbor leads to withdrawal of American relief organizations (JDC).	
Dec. 7 Riga massacre concluded (27 thousand).	

Events Outside Warsaw	Events in Warsaw
Dec. 11 Germany declares war on United States.	
Dec. 16 Frank reports about 2.5 million Jews in Government General must be "gotten rid of."	
	Dec. 17 German post office refuses to accept mail out of the ghetto using the excuse of epidemics.
Dec. 22 Vilna massacre completed (32 thousand).	
Dec. 30 Simferopol massacres completed (10 thousand) killed.	
Dec. 31 First permanent gassing camp opened at Chelmno, near Poznan (Posen).	

Events Outside Warsaw

Events in Warsaw

Dec.   Jewish cemetery walled off; coffins used for smuggling. Free soup kitchens supporting 100 thousand people.

1942

Jan.   Visits and tours of ghetto abolished for soldiers on leave, but they continue nevertheless.

Jan. 15 Resettlement operation begins in Lodz.

Jan. 31 A total 229,052 Jews reported killed in Baltic states and White Russia. First deportation to Teresienstadt.

Feb. 15 Singapore falls.

March 15 Hitler promises Russia will be annihilated in the summer.

March 16 Belzec death camp opens.

Events Outside Warsaw	Events in Warsaw
March 17-April 21 Most of Lublin ghetto resettled.	
Apr.-July Resettlement extends to whole of Poland.	
	April 12 Rumored arrival of extermination brigade.
	April 18 Bloody Friday execution of printers and distributors of ghetto undercover press. (Ringelblum blames Kohn and Heller.)
April 14 News of massacre at Lublin ghetto. News of pogroms in provinces.	
April 26 Reichstag approves Hitler's abrogation of German law.	
	May "The Thirteen" gang killed.

Events Outside Warsaw	Events in Warsaw
May 31 First of big air raids in Germany at Cologne.	
June News of massacres of Pabianice and Biala Podlaska.	
June 1 Jewish badge decreed in France and Holland.	
June 23 First gas chamber selection at train for Oswiecim (Paris).	
July Massacres extended to Minsk, Lida, Slonim, and Rovno.	
July 1 Germans reach El Alamein (Egypt), and the Don River (Russia).	

Events Outside Warsaw	Events in Warsaw
	July 22 A total of 380 thousand in Warsaw ghetto; Jewish Council publishes notice of deportation to East regardless of sex or age. Czerniakow commits suicide. By October 3, 310 thousand resettled.
	July 29 Meeting of Zionist youth organization decides to combine a unified striking force.
	July Zygmunt comes back with verified news of extermination camp at Treblinki.
Aug. 4 First deportation train from Belgium to Oswiecim.	

The Warsaw Ghetto Deportations, July 22, 1942

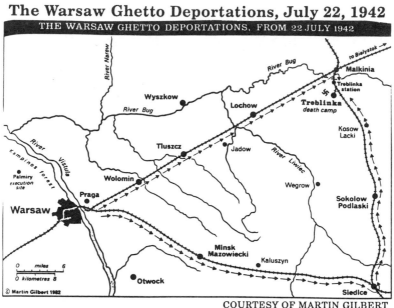

COURTESY OF MARTIN GILBERT

Distant Deportation, August 1942

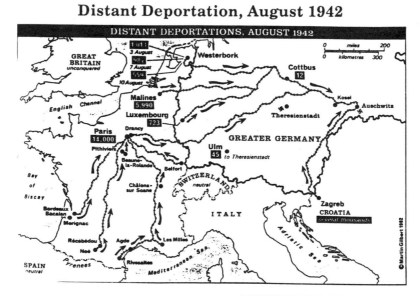

COURTESY OF MARTIN GILBERT

Events Outside Warsaw

Events in Warsaw

Aug. 5 Extermination squad descends on ghetto. The operation lasts a week.

Aug. 7 Blockade of every street and house begins.

Aug. 10-22 Forty thousand Jews resettled from Lwow (20 thousand left).

Mid-Aug. Germans in north Caucasus.

Aug. 19 Allies raid Dieppe.

Aug. 20 Jozef Szcrynski, head of Jewish police, badly wounded by assassin.

Aug. 26-28 Roundup of 7 thousand stateless Jews in Vichy Free Zone.

Aug. Hans Frank: "1.2 million Jews will no longer be provided with food."

Events Outside Warsaw	Events in Warsaw
Sept. 16 Lodz resettlement ends. Germans enter Stalingrad.	
	Sept. 21 Yom Kippur: Ghetto area reduced by more than half. More than three-quarters of population already evacuated. Two thousand Jewish policemen deported.
	Sept. 22 S.S. and S.D. take over formal administration of Jewish affairs in Warsaw.
Sept. 30 Hitler repeats prophecy of destruction of world Jewry.	
	Oct 3 First Warsaw resettlement ends.

Events Outside Warsaw	Events in Warsaw
Oct. 4 All Jews in concentration camps doomed to extermination at Oswiecim.	
Oct. 10 Ordinance lists thirteen ghettos and forty-two Jewish quarters in Government General.	
Oct. 14 Jews virtually outlawed from Holland.	
Oct. 18 Jews and "Easterners" in Reich given by Ministry of Justice to Gestapo.	
	Oct. 20 Coordinating Committee of resistance movement formed.
Oct. 28 End of first phase of Polish resettlement. More than 50 ghettos recognized.	
	Oct. 29 Jacob Lejkin, police officer, shot.

Events Outside Warsaw	Events in Warsaw
Oct. 29 Sixteen thousand Jews killed at Pinsk.	
Nov. 7 Allies land in North Africa.	
Nov. 11 Germans occupy Vichy France. Italians occupy Nice.	
Nov. 22 Russian counteroffensive begins.	
Nov. 26 Jewish munitions workers in Reich to be replaced by Poles.	
Dec. 17 United Nations declaration pledging punishment for extermination of Jewry.	
1943	
	Jan. Only 40,000 Jews left in the ghetto.
Jan. 14 Allies agreed on unconditional surrender at Casablanca meeting.	

Jan. 18 Second extermination operation begins. First resistance.

Feb. 2 German 6th army surrenders at Stalingrad.

Feb. 5-12 First resettlement from Bialaystok.

Feb. 15 Russians take Kharkov.

Feb. 27 Roundup of Jewish munitions workers in Berlin for Oswiecim.

March 13 Cracow ghetto liquidated. First of new crematoria opens at Oswiecim.

March 15 Deportations begin from Salonika and Thrace.

March Deportation trains from Holland to Sobibor death camp; those from Vienna, Luxembourg, Prague, and Maccedonia to Treblinki.

167

April 19-May 16
Liquidation of
the Warsaw
ghetto.
Uprising in
force. Ghetto
bombed, set
afire, razed. A
concentration
camp for two
thouand
Jewish and
Christian
prisoners
established on
site by SS.

Aug.   Russians advance.
Lodz's ghetto
survivors
transferred to
Oswiecim.

1944

March 7 Emanuel
Ringelblum
executed on
ruins of the
ghetto together
with wife and
child.

1946

Sept.   Ten cases of
Ringelblum
Archives dug
up.

1950

Dec. 1   Two
rubber-sealed
milk cans of
Ringelblum
Archives dug
up; documents
cover history
to March 1943.

Ghetto wall remnants can be found in the courtyard of Zlota 60 near Ulica Marchlewskiego in the vicinity of Holiday Inn Hotel. There is a plaque on the wall showing a map of the ghetto. Another remnant of the wall is at Ulica Sienna (Little Ghetto). Gestapo Headquarters Befehlsstelle Sipo at 103 Zelazna. Here the transports to Treblinka were planned. A plaque notes the building's history.

Zamenhof Memorial, in form of a plaque on the building at 5 Zamenhof St., honors Dr. Ludwik Zamenhof, the Bialystok physician who invented Esperanto in 1887 as an international language of peace. The plaque was dedicated in 1959, on the centennial of his birth, by the International Congress of Esperantists, to replace the monument erected in 1928 and destroyed by the Nazis. Zamenhof lived in Warsaw most of his adult life and is buried at the Warsaw Cemetery, where groups of Esperantists visit his grave. Zamenhof Street is world famous as the site of the ghetto uprising's birth.

Korczak Orphanage, at Ulica Jaktorowka 8 (92 Krochmalna Street), is named for Dr. Janusz Korczak (Henryk Goldszmit), physician, educator, and writer, who together with the children (whom he refused to abandon) from the Jewish orphanage he directed was killed by the Nazis. The building was designed in 1912 by Henryk Stiefelman. There is a plaque on the building as well as a small statute of Korczak in the courtyard and a plaque dedicated to the memory of the Polish janitor of the orphanage, Piotr Zalewski, shot by the Nazis in 1944.

Jewish Academic House (Auxilium Academicum Judaicum) in the Praga section of Warsaw at Ulica (Street)

Sierakowskiego 7 is presently used for local government offices. The letters AAJ are still visible on the building.

Jewish Historical Institute (founded in 1949) is located at 79 Aleja (Ave) Swierczewskiego (former Tlomackie 3/5) in the prewar building of the Judaic Institute and Central Library, designed by Edward Eber next door to the Great Synagogue on Tlomackie. The Jewish Historical Institute functions under the auspices of the Polish Academy of Sciences. It is open Monday through Friday from 9am to 3pm, and Saturday from 9am to noon.

Carrying out scientific research in the field of Jewish history, the institute deals with the history of Jews in Poland, and in other countries. The results of its research work are published in books and in *The Bulletin of the Jewish Historical Institute* in Poland, a quarterly periodical in Polish, with English and Yiddish summaries. They also publish a magazine in Yiddish entitled *Bletter far Geszichte* (Pages of History). The institute boasts of a library of over 50 thousand volumes dealing with Judaic and Semitic subjects; there are many unique old publications among them. Some of the manuscripts from the collections of about 1,000 items date from the tenth century. The institute also owns a collection of Jewish newspapers from the nineteenth century.

In the institute are rare records of the old Jewish communities, sets of documents dealing with the Nazi occupation and Jewish martyrdom, and files collected by Emanuel Ringelblum during his activities in the underground resistance movement.

Dr. Emanuel Ringelblum, a historian, organized an underground archives code-named "Oneg-Shabbat" in the early 1940s. The collection of documents describing the life and events of the Warsaw ghetto (1939-1943) was placed in milk cans and buried to avoid discovery by the Germans. They were found in 1946 and 1950 and now are the most important part of the permanent exhibition at the institute. These documents served as the basis of Dr. Ringelblum's historic writings, including *The Journal of Emanuel Ringelblum* and *Polish-Jewish Relations During the Second World War* (published by Yad Vashem).

The Judaica collection was assembled from the remnants
of Jewish libraries and museums looted by the Nazis
throughout Europe and then abandoned in a long line of
freight cars on a railroad siding in Silesia. The rescued
materials include manuscripts, books, and documents from
the Jewish theological seminaries in Wroclaw, Berlin, and
Vienna, as well as the famed rabbinic library of the Lublin
Yeshiva. Among the rare items on exhibit are a letter from
Spinoza's teacher; contemporary records of the Sabbatai Zvi
messianic movement in the seventeenth century; the minutes of the Council of the Four Lands (Va'ad Arbaa Aratzot)
in the seventeenth century; a ninth-century parchment diary of a Jewish traveler to Poland; and Jewish communal
archives from many Polish and Silesian towns.

The two upper floors, known as the Martyrs' Museum, are
entirely devoted to the story of the Warsaw getto, and the
other Polish ghettos. The most unusual exhibit consists of
two rusty milk cans in which Dr. Emanuel Ringelblum, the
archivist of the Warsaw ghetto, hid the daily record on the
life and death of Warsaw Jewry from 1939 to 1943. Above
the cans hangs a portrait of Dr. Ringelblum, who was shot
by the Nazis after the ghetto was destroyed. The cans were
dug up from under the ruins of a building on Nowolipie
Street in 1946. In these cans were diaries, reports, and
documents that survived because the cans were sealed
behind an armored, concrete-reinforced door. In another
can are an old hunting rifle and two pistols, part of the
weapons used by the ghetto fighters. Elsewhere are collected the records of the Jewish councils established by the
Nazis; files of ghetto newspapers, execution orders, and
statistics of arrivals and departures from the Warsaw
ghetto, files of the Warsaw branch of the American Jewish
Joint Distribution Committee to December 1941, and a
large gallery of photographs of life in the Warsaw ghetto
and paintings by ghetto artists. Also on display are por-
traits of World War II statesmen and leaders, including Dr.
Chaim Weizmann, Moshe Sharett, David Ben Gurion,
Stalin, Churchill, Roosevelt and Eisenhower.

On the thirty-fifth anniversary of the uprising, an exhibition entitiled "Art and Culture Behind the Walls" was cre-

MAP OF WARSAW JEWISH CEMETERY

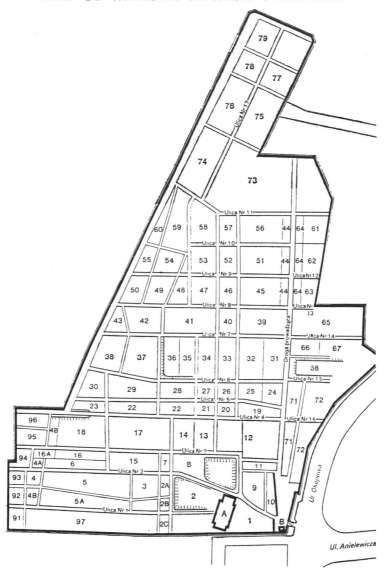

A - Mausoleum of rabbis
B - Prefuneral home
Numerals denote sections

ated, recognizing the talents of the murdered artists including Bruno Schultz, Efraim and Menasze Seidenbeutlow, Roman Kramsztyk, Henryk Glicenstein, Marcin Kitz, Maurycy Trebacz, Adolf Behrman, Mojzesz Rynecki, Geli Seksztajn, Jozef Kowner, Jonasz Stern, Jakub Glasner, and others.

The Grave of the Unknown Soldier, on the Pl. Zwyciestwa (Victoria Square) just across the street from the Victoria Hotel at the entrance to Saski Park, lists the Warsaw ghetto uprising among the major battles fought during World War II.

Kopciowka in Wilanow bears a plaque commemorating 67 Jews shot by the Germans in May 1944.

Praga-Polnoc bears a plaque at the southern railway station commemorating 600 Jews murdered by the Germans.

Wola has a plaque at the Jewish cemetery wall at Ulica (Street) Mlynarska 68 commemorating Jews shot in August 1944.

Warsaw Jewish Cemetery at 40 Okopowa Street at the end of Anielewicza Street miraculously survived the Nazi occupation. It is one of the oldest Jewish historic monuments in Warsaw. Established in 1799, it covers an area of 30 hectares and is divided into 100 sections containing two thouand graves.

It previously was the second Jewish cemetery in Warsaw, in addition to the one laid out in the Praga district in 1780. The latter was almost completely wiped out by the Nazis and overgrown with trees. In the Okopowa Street cemetery, currently in use, one can find splendid tombstones, some of them the works of famous sculptors, with rich ornaments in the shape of lions, deer, plants and trees. On the tombs belonging to priestly families (*kohanim*), hands joined in a gesture of blessing can be seen, while on those belonging to the levite families, there are hands holding a jug of water with which the priests' hands were sprinkled; a hand throwing a coin into an almsbox is the symbol of a philanthropist, while a hand holding a book appears on the tombs of scholars. In this cemetery are graves of famous politicians (such as S. Mendelson, and F. Perl), rabbis (Ber Meisels), scholars

(Samuel Dickstein, Ludwik Zamenhof [creator of Esperanto], Szymon Askenazy, Samuel Adalberg and Majer Balaban), and writers (Isaac Peretz, S. An-Ski, Dinesohn, and Ch.Z. Slonimski). Most of the graves face eastward toward Jerusalem.

The engravings on the stones are mainly in Hebrew, Yiddish, and Polish with some in Russian or German. Some of the gravestones are works of famous sculptors such as Dawid Frydlender, Mieczyslaw Lubelski, Abraham Ostrzega, Henryk Stifelman and others.

Some tent (*ohalim*) graves deserve special mention, such as the "Ohel" of Ber Sonnenberg (son of Szmul Zbytkower). Famous personalities including the Natansons, Epsteins, Toeplitzs, Wawelbergs, Rotwants, Szmul Zbytkower, Tugenhold, Isaac Kramsztyk and Samuel Orgelbrand, are buried here. There is also a section of graves of Jewish officers and men, soldiers of the Polish army, killed during the siege of Warsaw in 1939, and a mass grave of 300 unknown victims of the Nazis. There are gravestones of those who died in the Warsaw ghetto, including that of Adam Czerniakow, the president of the Jewish community (*Judenrat*), and his wife, Felicja. At the cemetery in 1988, Dr. Marek Edelman, the surviving member of the Warsaw Ghetto uprising command, dedicated at the Warsaw cemetery the symbolic grave of the leaders of Bund Henryk. Alter and Viktor Erlich (councilors of the city of Warsaw before World War II), who were executed by Stalin for their criticism of the Soviet invasion of Poland in 1939, are buried here. The cemetery is still in use and at present the grounds are being restored. present the cemetery grounds are being restored.

Famous figures in Polish Jewry Culture buried at the Warsaw Cemetery

Szymon AN-SKI (Salomon Zanwel RAPAPORT), 1863-1920

Writer and student of Jewish folklore, he wrote "Di shvue" (Oath), inspired by the 1905 revolution. This song came to be the hymn of Jewish socialists. In 1919 he published *Dybuk*, a moral drama, translated into several languages and played to the present day on many stages of the world. The collection of An-ski's works (15 volumes) was published in the interwar period in Warsaw.

The mausoleum was designed by Abraham Wstrzega.

Section 44, row 1 (common grave with J.L. Perec and I. Dinezon).

Szymon ASKENAZY,1867-1935

A historian and diplomat, Askenazy was a professor of the university in Lvov (Lwow) from 1904 to 1914. During World War I he was a member of the committee to help war victims in Polish lands; from 1920 to 1923 he was first Polish minister plenipotentiary to the League of Nations in Geneva. He was an expert on the history of Poland at the end of the eighteenth and the first half of the nineteenth centuries, and dealt with the history of international relations and diplomacy. In his works Askenazy expressed views on the vitality of the nation which was manifested in the stubborn fight for independence. His major works were *Ksiaze Jozef Poniatowski* (*Prince Jozef Poniatowski*), *Rosja,Polska 1815-1930* (*Russia, Poland 1815-1930*), *Lukasinski, Napoleon a Polska* (*Napoleon and Poland*). His treatise *Gdansk a Polska* (*Gdansk and Poland*), published in 1919 and translated into several languages, persuasively argued Poland's right to that town and seaport.

Section 10, row 6.

Majer BALABAN, 1877-1942

Balaban was a historian, pedagogue, publicist, professor of the Warsaw University, organizer and director of the Rabbinical School in Warsaw, and co-ordinator and rector of the Institute of Judaic Sciences. He popularized the history of Jews, with emphasis on the history of Jews in Poland. Balaban wrote in Polish, Yiddish, and Hebrew. Main works include *Dzieje Zydow w Krakowie i na Kazimierzu 1304-1868* (*The History of Jews in Cracow and in Kazimierz 1304-1868*), *Zabytki historyczne Zydow w Polsce* (*Historical Relics of Jews in Poland*), and a three-volume work entitled *Historia i literatura Zydowska* (*Jewish History and Literature*), and *Bibliografia historii Zydow w Polsce w latach*

1990-1930 (Bibliography of the History of Jews in Poland in the Years 1900-1930).
Section 9, row 10.

Michael BERGSON, 1831-1919

Bergson was a social worker, philanthropist, and descendant of Szmul Zbytkower, who founded the Jewish cemetery in the suburb of Praga. He served as president of the Community of Orthodox Jews in Warsaw from 1986 to 1918 and was active in many social associations, including the agricultural school for youth in Czestoniew near Grojec. He founded the Jewish educational and institutions at Jagiellonska Street in Warsaw.
Section 33, row 10.

Majer BERSOHN, 1787-1873

Bersohn was the senior memeber of a philanthropists and social workers organization, founder of the hospital for children at Sliska Street bearing the name of the Bersohns and Baumans (now the Hospital of the Children of Warsaw), and founder of the rabbinical school, and Jewish hospital.
Section 26, row 2.

Mathias BERSOHN, 1824-1908

Bersohn developed a sizable collection of works of art and culture, which he donated in 1904 to the Jewish community. They became the nucleus of the Museum of Jewish Antiquities which was named after him. The remaining collections were later taken over by the National Museum in Warsaw. Bersohn was an author of many works on the subject of Art and Culture.
Section 26, row 2.

Section of Bund fighters in Warsaw ghetto

There is a collective monument to the ghetto fighters of BUND and CIKUNFT, the youth organization of that party.

Gabriel CENTNERSZWER, 1841-1917

Centnerszwer was a bookseller, publisher, and participant in the 1863 insurrection. He published more than 200 books. On his initiative the first Polish language primer for Jewish children appeared.

Adam CZERNIAKOW, 1880-1942

An engineer, and political and social activist, Czerniakow was president of the Central Union of Jewish Craftsmen; senator of the Republic in the years 1931-1935, and chairman of the Jewish Religious Community. At the time of occupation (until July 1942) he served as president of the Council of Elders (Judenrat) and administrative institution formed by Nazis to execute order of the occupants. On July 22, 1942, he was forced by the Gestapo to sign the deportation order of Jews. He committed suicide as a sign of protest, realizing that they would be sent to extermination camps. On his monument is a fragment of Norwid's composition, "What have you done to Athens?" and a quotation from the Book of Ezekiel (16:6) in Hebrew.

Section 10, row 3-4.

Samuel DICKSTEIN, 1851-1939

Dickstein was a mathematician, science historian, professor of the Warsaw University, author of many works, and member of scientific societies in Poland and abroad. He served as superintendent of the M. Bersohn Museum of the Jewish community.

Antoni EISENBAUM, 1791-1852

Director of the Rabbinical School in Warsaw, Eisenbaum was an advocate of the Haskala enlightenment movement. In the years 1823 to 1824 he edited the *Dostrzegacz Nadwislanski (Der Beobachter an der Weichsel)*, a periodical in German in which he advocated equal rights for the Jewish population.

Section 1, row 2.

Jakub EPSTEIN, 1771-1843

Forefather of a well-known family of industrialists and businessmen, Epstein was a participant in the Kosciuszko insurrection. He was a protector and contributor to the building of the Jewish hospital and synagogue at Danilowiczowska Street.

Section 9, row 10.

Leon FEINER, 1885-1945

A lawyer, Feiner was a Bund activist in Cracow before World War II. During the occupation he assumed the pseudonym Mikolak,and acted as vice chairman of the Council for Help to Jews, 'Zegota,'an underground organization created by the government representation in the homeland to help Jews who went into hiding.

BUND Section at the Main Alley.

Azriel Natan FRENK, 1863-1924

A publicist and historian, Frenk co-operated with Polish and Hebrew periodicals. He authored historical studies *Wojny Napoleonskie* (*Napoleonic Wars*), *Z przeszlosci zydowstwa warszawkiego* (*From the Past of Warsaw Jewry*), *and Z dziejow cenzury ksiag zydowskich* (*A Contribution to the History of Censorship of Jewish Books*). He translated Boleslaw Prus's *Faraon* (*The Pharaoh*), and Henryk Sienkiewicz's *Ogniem i mieczem* (*With Fire and Sword*), and H. Sienkiewicz's *Potop (The Deluge)* into Yiddish.

Section 44, row 1.

Pawel GOLDKRAUT, 1898-1978

A civil engineer, Godlkraut served in the Polish Military Organization during World War I. After 1945 he participated in the reconstruction of many buildings in Warsaw and other cities. Goldkraut co-operated in the construction of the building at Plac Grzybowski (Grzybowski Square) in Warsaw, now the seat of the Headquarters of the Social and Cultural Society of Jews in Poland, and of the Jewish Theater. He was a member of the Board of Directors of the Jewish Historical Institute in Poland.

Section 10, row 5.

Estera Rachel KAMINSKA, 1870-1925

Known as the mother of Jewish theater, Kaminska made her acting debut in 1888, and performed in many countries. In 1913 she founded the Jewish Theater in Warsaw, naming it after her husband Abraham Kaminiski. She was the mother of Esther Kaminski and aunt of Danny Kaye. In 1955 the State Jewish Theater in Warsaw was named after

her. The monument at her grave was designed by Feliks
Rubinlicht.
Section 39, row 1.

Michael KLEPFISZ, 1913-1943

An engineer and leading activist of the underground
BUND in the Warsaw ghetto, Klepfisz was a representative
of the Jewish Fighting Organization in the Polish resis-
tance movement. He was killed during the ghetto uprising.
(There is a symbolic monument.)
Section 20 main alley.

Janusz KORCZAK, pen name of Henryk GOLDSZMIT, 1878-1942

A doctor, educator and writer of children's books, Korczak
is best known for "King Matt The First." Before World War
II he established and ran a Jewish orphanage in Warsaw,
edited the children's newspaper "Maly Przeglad" (Little Re-
view) and ran a radio program for children. After decling
offers to be rescued, he marched with his children on August
5, 1942, to Umschlagplatz and perished in Treblinka. A
symbolic monument designed by Mieczslaw Smorczewski
stands parallel to Okopowa Street.
Section 72

Izaak KRAMSZTYK, 1814-1889

Kramsztyk was a preacher, publicist, and founder of the
first reform synagogue in Warsaw (1852). He preached in
Polish and participated in anti-Russian rallics on the eve of
the January Insurrection in 1863. He appealed for active
solidarity of Jews with the insurgents and was punished for
this by exile into Russia. Kramsztyk later cooperated with
papers appearing in Polish addressed to the Jewish population in which he propagated the ideas of progress and
tolerance.
Section 20, row 12

Michael LANDY, 1844-1861

Landy was a participant in the anti-tsarist rally at Plac
Zamkowy (Castle Square) in Warsaw on April 8, 1861. He
was shot the moment he took up the cross held by another

protestor who fell dead at his side. His death inspired a number of poets and painters, among them Artur Szyk. Section 20, row 12.

Bernard MARK, 1908-1966

Mark was a historian and publicist. In People's Poland he was an editor of periodicals published by the Social and Cultural Society of Jews in Poland, and served as director of the Jewish Historical Institute from 1949 to 1966. He wrote about the resistance movement in ghettos, particularly in the Warsaw ghetto uprising. Section 64, row 1.

Abraham MOREWSKI,1886-1964

Morewski was an actor and stage manager in the Jewish theater in Vilna, and later in the United States. After the Nazi armies invaded the Soviet Union, he acted for approximately 12 years on Russian stages. In 1956 he returned to Poland, where he became one of the leading actors of the Kaminska Theater. Section 64, row 1.

Zelig Samuel NATANSON, 1705-1879

The head of the family, Natanson was a banker, industrialist, and co-founder of the Great Synagogue in Warsaw. Several of his sons played important roles in the cultural and scientific life of the country. Section 20, Rows 7

Samuel ORGELBRAND, 1810-1868

Orgelbrand was a publisher and bookseller. From 1842 to 1850 he published *Kmiotek* (Rustic), the first paper in Poland for country people. His crowning achievement was the 28-volume *Encyklopedia Powszechna* (Universal Encyclopaedia). He published *Talmud Babilonski* (*The Babylonian Talmud*) in Hebrew. Section 20, row 7.

Icchak Leib PEREC, 1852-1915

Perec was a writer, dramatist, and lawyer. After his youthful poetical attempts in Polish and Hebrew, he wrote the poem *Monisz* (in Yiddish in an innovative style) in 1888.

He wrote short stories on social problems, which were published in the collection *Folksimliche geszichten* (*Country-Folk Tales*). The plot of the poem *Chsydisz* (*The World of Rabbinists*) was based on Orthodox Jewish customs. His dramas "Baj nacht pjfn alten mark" (By Night on the Old Market Square), and "Di goldene kajt" (Golden Chain) have always been stock pieces in Jewish theaters all over the world. His numerous novels, satirical compositions, and comprehensive publicism combining modern European thought with Polish national tradition and folklore put Perec among the greats of literature in Yiddish. His *Kpiarz* (*Scoffer*), a selection of satirical novels written in 1888, and a collection of short stories (1958) were translated into Polish.

This monument was designated by Abraham Ostrzega (1924).

Section 44, row 1 (common grave with An-ski and Dinezon).

Feliks PERL, 1871-1927

Co-founder of the Polish Socialist Party, Perl was its leading theoretician, publicist, and chief editor of the party's main organ *Robotnik* (*Worker*). He was a member of the Sejm (Parliament) Mieczyslaw Niedzialkowski, celebrated activist of the party said at Perl's grave: "There is no Polish socialist in whom the cause of independence and socialism would be fused to such an extent as in Perl."

Section 24, row 2

Zofia ROSENBLUM-SZYMANSKA, 1888-1978

Rosenblum-Szymanska was a doctor, and co-originator of medical attention stations for children. From 1928 to 1939 she was head of such a station in Otwock near Warsaw. In the Warsaw ghetto she was chief doctor (until 1942) of a number of pediatric stations. After liberation she became the head of a dispensary for underdeveloped children at the Institute of Mental Hygiene. She participated in international congresses as a delegate of the Ministry of Health and authored several popular science works.

Section 67, row 5.

Chaim Zelig SLONIMSKI, 1810-1904

Slonimski was a mathematician, astronomer, and inventor. He improved the computing machine co-invented by Abraham Stern, his father-in-law. In 1862 in Warsaw he founded the first popular science journal in Hebrew *Ha-cefira* (*Dawn*). He was the grandfather of Antoni Slonimski, poet and publicist.
Section 71, row 1.

Ber SONNENBERG, 1764-1822

A merchant and entrepreneur, Sonnenberg founded the synagogue in the suburb of Praga. Son of Szmul and popularly known as "Zbytkower," Ber was a banker, owner of many houses and building lots in Praga, founder of the Jewish cemetery in that quarter, and a personage invested in a mantle of legend dating from the period of the Kosciuszko insurrection. Descendants of Ber assumed the name of Bergson. One of them, philosopher and writer Henri Bergson who lived in France from 1859 to 1941, won the Nobel Prize in literature (1927).

Hipolit WAWELBERG, 1844-1901

A financier, philanthropist and social worker, Wawelberg initiated popular editions of works by most prominent Polish writers and poets and financed the foundation called "Cheap Apartments in Warsaw." Together with his brother-in-law, Stanislaw Rotwand, he founded the High Technical School (bearing their names) in 1891, which was incorporated in 1951 with the Warsaw Technical University. Wawelberg founded the building that housed the Museum of Industry and Trade. A street in Warsaw near the blocks of flats for workers financed from his foundation was named after him.
Section 20, row 3.

Ludwik ZAMENHOF, 1859-1917

An opthamologist, Zamenhof was the creator of a universial (Esperanto) language, the first handbook of which appeared in 1887 in Warsaw. He assumed the pseudonym "Doktoro Esperanto" after which his language was named. The main source of inspiration in the creation of Esperanto was misunderstandings on nationalistic grounds in his native city Bialystok. In the universal language Zamenhof saw the possibility of making unrestricted contacts between people of various nationalities. He translated into Esperanto a number of works of world literature. According to approximate data this language is now being used by 2.5 million people all over the world.

His monument was designed by Mieczyslaw Lubelski. Section 10, row 2.

Mass graves of Warsaw Jews from the ghetto years 1941-1942 have now been partially identified.

Monument to Soldiers of the Polish Army who fell in defense of Warsaw in September 1939. Out of the total of one million Polish Army members fighting the German invasion of September 1939, about 100 thousand Jews were called up. According to historian Filip Friedman, 32 thousand were killed in action and 61 thousand were taken prisoners of war.

Jewish Cemetery at Brodno, in the Prague district of Warsaw across the Wisla (Vistula) River, was established in 1780 by Szmul Zbytkower (Jozef Samuel Jukubowicz). The cemetery contains 300 thousand graves and was nearly destroyed by the Germans. The cemetery was established on a piece of land in what was known as Targowek. It was donated to Szmul Zbytkower (also buried here) by King Stanislaus Augustus Poniatowski, the last King of Poland. One well-known person buried in the cemetery is Abraham Stern, an inventor of the mathematical calculating machine.

The cemetery is presently being restored mainly through the efforts of the Nissenbaum Foundation.

At the **Polish Army Military** cemetery are some Jewish graves of soldiers killed in action in defense of Warsaw in September 1939. Also an obelisk in a form of a matzeva commemorates 6500 Jews shot at the sports field **"Skra."**

Wilanow, on the road to Powsina, is an obelisk honoring 67 Jews shot by the Germans in May 1944.

Warta

The Jews came to Warta in the thirteenth century. The first synagogue was built in 1534. Jews of Warta enjoyed rich political life including Bund and Zionist movements. They were also active in the Polish independence movement in the nineteenth century and a few even suffered deportation to Siberia. There were two thousand Jews in Warta on the eve of World War II.

In May 1942 the Germans executed a number of Jewish inhabitants, including the heroic Rabbi Laskowski. The remnants perished in Chelmno.

The cemetery at Ulica Gorna 7 was completely destroyed. The cemetery at Ulica Sadowa features 170 matzevot. The synagogue is now living quarters.

Wasosz

Mass grave of 250 Jews shot by the Wehrmacht in August 1941 is here.

Wesola

A monument to the Jews of the area shot in the fields in August 1942 is here.

Wieliczka

Jews of Wieliczka (about 1300) together with those of the area, some 8 thousand in total, were deported to Belzec and a small minority to labor camps in Plaszow and Stalowa Wola.

The cemetery in Grabowka area still features 50 mazevot, as well as mass graves.

A monument honors the victims of the Holocaust at the Jewish cemetery at Siercza.

Wielkie Oczy

The synagogue is now a silo. The cemetery has a few matzevot and a tablet for 41 Jews shot by the German Gendarmerie.

Wielki Gleboczek (Brzozie Parish)

Memorial tablet on the wall of the school located on the grounds of labor camp honors Jewish women who perished there. The camp was liquidated in January 1945.

Wielun

Jews came to Wielun in the sixteenth century. By 1939 the community consisted of 4200 persons. Most of them perished in Chelmno. An obelisk honors the victims of Shoa. The cemetery at Ulica Kijok 17, was completely destroyed.

Wieruszow

There were about three thousand Jews here before the war. Most of them perished in Chelmno.

A commemorative plaque honoring victims of Wieruszow ghetto, is located at the Jewish cemetery, (with 200 matzevot).

Wiewiorka

An obelisk honors 18 people murdered on March 23, 1943; they were accused by the Germans of assisting the partisans and hiding Jews.

Wiszenki

A tablet marks the execution place of 30 people accused of helping Jews and Soviet POWs.

Wlodawa

There were nearly six thousand Jews in Wlodawa on the eve of World War II. Most of its inhabitants perished in Sobibor. There was a Jewish partisan unit in the area under the command of Yehiel Grynszpan.

For nearly 50 years, the synagogue in Wlodawa has been in ruins. Destroyed during the Holocaust, it has recently been rebuilt through private contributions. It will house a permanent exhibition of Judaica, featuring articles taken from Wlodawa's Jewish residents.

The cemetery at Ulica Wiejska was nearly destroyed.

Wodzislaw

There is a grave at the Jewish cemetery for victims of the German executions, that took place in September and October 1943.

The sixteenth-century synagogue was abandoned.

Wolbrom

The Jewish community of Wolbrom consisted of five thousand people. A ghetto existed from 1941 until September 1942, when the Germans killed two thousand people. The remainder were deported to Belzec.

There is a mass grave at the Jewish cemetery for victims of the area.

Wroclaw (Breslau)

The Jewish community of Wroclaw dates back to the twelth century. In the 1930s (prior to World War II), this German city was already exposed to Nazi atrocitices. During the *Kristalnacht* the Nazis burned and demolished houses of prayer as well as living quarters.

During 1941 the Jews of Wroclaw were deported to the Riga ghetto and Terezin camp in Czechoslovakia. A sizable Jewish community emerged after World War II when some Jews repatriated from the Soviet Union and settled there in what was German territory ceded to Poland. The community was vastly depleted by waves of emigration in the 1950s and finally 1968.

Today there is a Jewish community of about 1,000 (large by today's Polish standards) in Wroclaw, a town that became part of Poland after World War II. Only about ten percent of the Jewish population are young people.

There is a **Jewish community center** and neoclassical (Pod Bialym Bocianem-Storch) synagogue built in 1827 by architect Karol Gotthard at Wlodkowica 9, as well as a kosher kitchen that dispenses about 60 meals a day. The **Jewish Hospital** Israelitisches Kraukenhaus, built in 1726 and located at Ulica Wisniowa, is now a railroad hospital.

A **Jewish cemetery** at Slezna and Sztabowa streets contains some great specimens of gravestone art from the nineteenth century. Some famous members of the Wroclaw community are buried here, including

Heinrick Graetz, a famous historian; Ferdinand Lassale, a leader of the German Labor Movement and a participant in the "Spring of Nations"; Jan Gotfryd Gallea, discoverer of planet Neptune; and Max Moszkowski, explorer of Sumatra.

Cemetery at Ulica Lotnicza 51 has some 8000 graves.

At the Plac (Square) Grunwaldzki, a **memorial** commemorates murdered Polish scientists and men of letters, including some Jews (Boy-Zelenski). The murder took place in Lvov (Lwow) in the summer of 1941. The monument contains earth from the place of the execution.

Plac Bohaterow Ghetta was named for the heroes of the ghetto. A Warsaw ghetto monument is nearby.

Wroclawek

At the communal cemetery, there are 24 individual and three mass graves, one of which contains remains of Jews from the Rakutowek ghetto.

Wrzesnia

A gravestone at the western part of the railway station honors the victims of labor camp for Jews called "Julag."

Zablotczyzna

Mass grave of 500 Jews murdered on August 5, 1941, is here.

Zabno

Mass graves of approximately 100 Jews murdered by the Nazis on March 11 and 12, 1942, are here; also a cemetery.

Zagorow

A monument honors freedom fighters at Pl. (Square) Maciejewskiego, and also honors 2,500 Jews from the ghetto shot in October 1941, in the woods of Kazimierz Biskupi. The cemetery was destroyed.

Zagorz

A memorial at the mass grave Ulica (Street) Fabryczna marks where four thousand victims of the Holocaust were executed at the camp between 1940 and 1944.

Zamosc

On the eve of World War II 60 percent of this eastern

city's population was Jewish. A synagogue was built in the sixteenth century and some community organizations were established.

In the eighteenth century Sephardic Jews came into town. The eighteenth and nineteenth centuries witnessed the introduction of a variety of Jewish political and religious movements.

Some famous personalities are identified with Zamosc. Among them are Rabbi Zvi Hirsh, Rabbi Yacov Krantz (known as "Hamagid from Dubna") Rabbi Isaac Zamosc and famous literary figure Icchak Leib Perec.

A synagogue was built in the early seventeenth century on the basis of a "privilege" granted the Jews in 1588. It is in the Post-Renaissance style; it was destroyed during the German occupation and rebuilt between 1950 and 1965 in its original form including stucco work and murals. The synagogue stands in a neighborhood with streets named after Dr. Zamenhof and Perec, who was born there. At present, the synagogue houses a library.

A monument honors prisoners of the transit camp used by the Germans during the deportation from Zamosc.

The "Rotunda" houses the Museum of Martyrology of Zamosc. It is located at the place of mass executions of Jews, Poles and Russian POWs.

A plaque at an agricultural school, which was used as an S.S. riding school, commemorates Jews and POWs who worked there.

A monument commemorates 10 thousand Jews of Zamosc murdered in the ghetto and Belzec camp.

A plaque at the Stara Brama Lubelska commemorates hundreds of Jews, Poles and Russian POWs shot by the German gendarmes on the premises of Zamoyskiego High School.

A monument at Ulica (Street) Szedzka honors Russian POWs, from 1943 POW camp there. The Wehrmacht shot on arrival any Jewish POW as well as any political officers.

A monument in the woods of Rapy marks the place of execution of Jews and partisans who were executed by the Germans in 1944.

PLAN OF ZAMOSC

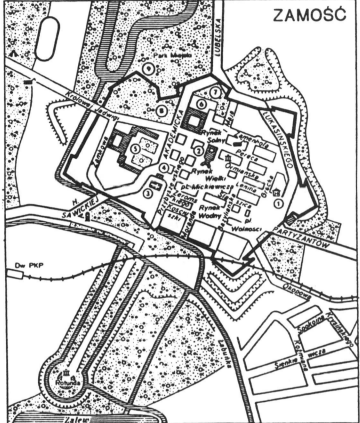

Zary

A Jewish community and house of worship is at Armii Czerwonej 3A.

Zarzecze

Monument here honors the inmates of labor camp for Czech and Austrian Jews.

Zarki

Even though there were only 600 Jews in Zarki, the community had a high school and library founded by Abraham Joseph Sztybel featuring a collection of six thousand books.

The cemetery at Ulica Polna has 900 matzevot. It was cleaned up and renovated through the efforts of Eli Zborowski from New York. The nineteenth-century synagogue was renovated in 1950 and is now used as a culture house.

Zaslow

The Martyrs Memorial honors ten thousand Jews, Poles and Gypsies murdered by the Nazis in the nearby Sanok concentration camp.

Zbylitowska Gora

The mausoleum in the woods of Buczyna honors some ten thousand people, among them 800 Jewish children murdered in the woods. The mausoleum itself marks the mass grave and the spot of the executions in the years 1942-1944.

Zdroj

An obelisk commemorates 1,400 Jews shot on August 10, 1942.

Zdunska Wola

Community is relatively new, established only in the nineteenth century. However by 1939, ten thousand (40 percent) of the inhabitants were Jewish.

The community had its synagogue, Hebrew schools and banking cooperative. The cemetery (established in 1858) at Ulica Kacza features approximately 400 graves. The synagogue built in 1858 near the railway station is now used for storage.

Zgierz

There is a cemetery at intersection of Barona and Plaskowa streets.

Zolkiewka

A monument honors Jews from the Zolkiewka ghetto.

Zwiernik

There is a grave of three Jews and the Pole who hid them all shot by the Germans in 1943.

Zwolen

The community dates back to 1554. By the outbreak of World War II there were 3800 Jews in Zwolen (51 percent of the population);most of them perished in the labor camps at Puskowic or Treblinka.

A monument to the victims of terror at Pl. Kochanowskie commemorates 500 Poles and Jews shot by the German gendarmes on June 17, 1944.

APPENDIX I

Congregations and Synagogues

Congregation	Synagogue	House of Worship
Bielsko-Biala Mickiewicza 26		Mickiewicza 26
Bytom Smolenska 4	Pl. Grunwaldski 62	
Chrzanow		Chajnowska 16
Czestochowa Garibaldiego 18		Garibaldiego 18
Dzierzoniow Krasickiego 28	Krasickiego 28	
Gliwice Dolne Waly 9		Dolne Waly 9
Katowice Mlynska 13		Mlynska 13

Krakow (Cracow) Remu
Skawinska 2 Szeroka 49
 Templum
 Miodowa 24

Legnica Chajnowska 17
Chajnowska 17

Lodz Rewolucji 1905 r. 28 Zachodnia 78
Zachodnia 78

Lublin Lubartowska 10
Lubartowska 10

Nowy Sacz Jagielonska 12

Swidnica Bohaterow Getta 22

Przyrow Leloska 2

Szczecin Niemcewicza 2
Niemcewicza 2

Walbrzych Mickiewicza 18
Mickiewicza 18

Wroclaw (Breslau) Wlodkowica 9
Wlodkowicza 9

Warszawa Nozyka
Twarda 6 Twarda 6

Zgorzelec Boh. Getta 3
Boh. Getta 3

Zary k. Zagania Armii Czerwonej 3A
Armii Czerwonej 3A

APPENDIX II

Jewish Organizations

Name and Address	Phone
American-Polish Foundation for Polish-Jewish Culture Plac Grzybowski 12/16 00-104 Warsaw	20-05-09
International Janusz Korczak Society (Miedzynarodowe Stowarzyszenie Im. Janusza Korczaka) Sniadeckich 17 00-654 Warsaw	29-52-09
Israel Embassy Krzywickiego 24 02-078 Warsaw	25-09-23 25-00-28
Jagiellonian University- Research Center on Jewish History and Culture in Poland	22-10-33 Ext. 143, 183

(Uniwersytet Jagiellonski -
Miedzynarodowy Zaklad
Nauki i Kultury Zydow w Polsce)
UL. Batorego 12
31-135 Cracow

Jewish Cemetery (Cmentarz Zydowski)   38-26-22
4951 Okopowa
01-043 Warsaw

Jewish Cultural and Social Union   20-62-81
(Towarzystwo Kulturalne Zydow w Polsce)
Plac Grzybowski 12/14
00-104 Warszawa

Jewish Historical Institute   27-18-43
(Zydowski Instutut Historyczny)
Aleje Tlomackie
00-090 Warszawa

Jewish Newspaper   20-05-49
(Folks-Sztym)   20-62-81
Plac Grzybowski 12/14
00-104 Warsaw

Jewish Religious Organization   20-43-24
(Zwiazek Religijny Wyznania Mojzeszowego) 20-06-76
Twarda 6
00-950 Warsaw

Jewish State Theater   20-49-54
(Panstwowy Teatr Zydowski   20-70-25
Im. Estery Kaminskiej)
Plac Grzybowski 12/16
00-104 Warsaw

Nissenbaum Family Foundation   24-14-77
Ulica Twarda 6
00-105 Warsaw

Polish Association of Righteous Gentiles   29-52-09
(Polskie Towarzystwo Sprawiedliwych)
c/o Miedzynarodowe
Stowarzyszenie Im.
Janusza Korczaka
Sniadeckich 17
00-654 Warsaw

Polish-Israel Friendship League
c/o Cafe Eilat
Aleje Ujazdowskie 47
Warsaw

Public Committee for Protection of   29-62-26
   Jewish Cemeteries and Endowments
(Spoleczny Komitet Opieki Nad Cmentarzami)
1 Zabykami Kultury Zydowskiej W Polsce
Ulica Piekna 44S
00-672 Warsaw

The Ronald S. Lauder Foundation   20-05-56
Plac Grzybowski 12/16
00-104 Warsaw

APPENDIX III

Practical Information

Cracow (Krakow)
AIRPORT:Balice DRK, ten miles northwest of the city.

Warsaw
AIRPORT:Okecie, 28 Marii Konopnickiej WAW, 6 miles southwest of the city.
Scheduled airlines/reservation telephone numbers:
El Al: 30 66 16/7/8
LOT: 21 70 21   LUFTHANSA: 89 51 277
SWISS AIR: 27 50 16   KLM: 75 93 600

Baggage

The "piece concept" that prevails on transatlantic flights does not apply to intra-European flights or Europe to Israel flights where the airlines can apply 44-pound limits. Please keep this in mind when packing. If your stay in Eastern Europe is very short, lost luggage can present a considerable inconvenience. We highly recommend that you carry with you toiletries, a change of undergarments and medications in an overnight bag. Make sure luggage tags with your name and phone number are well affixed to your suitcase.

mate

Countrywide Average

	Jan	Feb	Mar	Apr	May	June	July	Aug	Sept	Oct	Nov	Dec
Average Low (F)	23°	24°	30°	37°	47°	51°	56°	54°	49°	40°	32°	27°
Average High (F)	32°	35°	43°	54°	67°	72°	74°	73°	65°	54°	42°	35°
Warsaw Average Rainfall (in inches)	1	1	1	2	2	3	3	3	2	2	1	1

Communications

When dialing direct to Poland, dial the proper international access code: (011 from the United States) plus 48 (country code) plus city code (see individual city listings) plus local number. There is a wait for overseas telephone calls in Warsaw. One way to get around the problem is to send a telex home asking those at home to call you using direct dial from the United States. Don't forget to give your room number.

Recently an AT&T access number was introduced. You may reach the U.S. operator by dialing:

WARSAW:010-480-0111(POLAND)
POLAND:(outside Warsaw)0-DIAL TONE-010-480-0111

When transmitting telex messages from the United States, the code 867 (for Poland) must precede the telex number.

Fax machines have been introduced recently in Poland but reliability is a problem.

Currency

The Polish monetary unit is the zloty, divided into 100 groszy.

Coins are issued in 1, 2, 5, 10, 20 zlotys and 10, 20 and 50 groszy. Bills are issued in 10, 20, 50, 100, 200, 500, 1000, 2000 and 5000 zlotys. Currency conversion rate at press time is $1 U.S. = ZL.9500.

Currency regulations once strictly enforced have been greatly liberalized lately, and foreign currency can be changed at practically free market rates. Incidentally, it will save time if you know the exact amount of money you are carrying and converting before arriving in Warsaw. You should also register your gold jewelry, leather and furs upon arrival. It is important to guard your currency declaration carefully, as you might be required to present it on departure.

Electricity

Electrical appliances run on 220 volts, at 50 cycles. A plug adapter and a converter are necessary for all electrical appliances and equipment.

Embassies

Canada: Ul. Matejki 1/5, 00-481, Warsaw Tel: 29 80 51.

Great Britain: Al Roz 1, 00-556, Warsaw Tel: 38 100
    1/05(days) and 628 100 1/02(nights).

Great Britain Consulate: Ul Wawelska 14, 02-061, War-
    saw. Tel: 6288-31/35

Israel: Krzywickiego 24, 02-078, Warsaw Tel: 6250923,
    250028.

United States: Aleje Ujazdowskie 29/31, Warsaw, Tel:
    283041/9.

U.S. Consulate: Krakow, Ulica Stolarska 9, 31043,
    Krakow Tel: 229764.

Hotels

Cracow (Krakow)

Forum Hotel: 28 Marii Konopnickiej, Tel: 669500, Tlx:
    0322737.

Holiday Inn Hotel: Ul. Koniewa 7, Tel: 375044, Tlx:
    0325356.

Warsaw

Europejski Hotel: Ul. Krakowskie Przedmiescie 13, Tel:
    26 50 51, Tlx: 81 36 15.

Forum Hotel-Warsaw: Nowogrodzka 24/26, Tel: 21 02 71,
    Tlx: 81 47 04.

Holiday Inn: Ul. Zlota 2, Tel: 20 03 41, Tlx: 81 74 18 or 81
    77 78.

Marriot Hotel: Aleje Jerozolimskie 65/79, Tel: 30 63 06, Tlx: 81 65 14, Fax: 48 22 21.
Victoria Inter Continental Hotel: Ul. Krolewska 11, Tel: 27 80 11, Tlx: 81 25 16, Fax: 279856.

Kosher Food

There is no way to obtain kosher food in Poland, with the exception of an occasional meal at the JDC-supported canteens in Warsaw or Cracow, and the newly established Menorah restaurant in Warsaw at Plac Grzybowski; those observing *kashrut* should bring food with them. Following are some suggestions of items you may want to include:

Cans of tuna with flip-tops (small cans of gefilte fish with flip-tops).
Boxes of matzah, if "motzei" is desired.
Vacuum-packed plastic packages of meat.
Cans of fruit, such as sliced peaches or pears.
Small bottles of wine or grape juice, if "Kiddush" is desired.
Two forks, two spoons, two knives - one set for dairy, one set for meat.
Can opener or Swiss army knife.
Granola bars, nuts or dried fruit.
Can of sardines.
Crackers.
Salami.
Yahrzeit and Shabbat candles.
Paper plates, napkins, and plastic sandwich bags.

Shopping

There is a rather limited number of items of Jewish interest available in Poland. At times you will be able to find books on Jewish subjects at bookstores. These include *Polish Jewry*, and *Time of Stones*, both now available in English. Some other books on Judaica are also available in Polish, as well as works of Janusz Korczak. The Jewish Historical Institute has a considerable number of publications, mainly in Polish but also in Yiddish and English.

Occasionally you will find a Pewex (duty-free shop); at tourist hotels or philatelic stores, a sterling silver coin commemorating Janusz Korczak or Ludwik Zamenhof may be available. In Cracow's Sukiennice (shopping mall), the first folklore stand has wood carvings of chasidim.

Time

Poland is six hours ahead of U.S. Eastern Standard Time. Banking hours are from 8am to noon or 2pm, Monday through Saturday. Business hours are from 8am to 3pm. Shopping hours are from 9am to 3pm (department stores); from 6am to 6pm (food stores); and 11am to 7pm (shops). Check with a concierge for the weekend hours.

Tobacco and Liquor

Import allowances for tobacco are one carton of cigarettes or 50 cigars or 8 3/4 oz. of tobacco for travelers 18 years of age or older. Liquor allowances are one liter for travelers 17 years of age or older. There is little need to bring tobacco or liquor into the country. There is a duty-free store (Pewex) at some hotels; they usually are well stocked with popular brands of liquor and cigarettes.

APPENDIX IV

Recommended Reading

Arad, Yitzkhak, *Ghetto in Flames*. Yad Vashem.

Bauer, Yehuda, *The Holocaust in Historical Perspective*. University of Washington.

Bartoszewski, Wladyslaw, *The Ghetto: A Christian's Testimony*. Beacon Press.

Conot, Robert, *Justice at Nuremberg*. Carrol & Graf.

Czerniakow, Adam, *The Warsaw Diary of Adam Czerniakow*. Stein and Day.

Davidowicz, Lucy, *The War Against the Jews*. Holt, Rinehart, and Winston.

Dobroszycki, Lucjan, *The Chronicle of the Lodz Ghetto 1941-1944*. Yale University Press.

Frank, Anne, *The Diary of a Young Girl*. Pocket Books.

Friedlander, Albert, *Out of the Whirlwind: A Holocaust Anthology*. Schocken.

Fuks, Marian, Zygmunt Hoffman, Maurycy Horn, and Jerzy Tomaszewski, *The Polish Jewry*. Interpress-Warsaw.

Gilbert, Martin, *Auschwitz and the Allies*. Holt, Rinehart, and Winston.

Gilbert, Martin, *The Holocaust*. Fontana/Collins.

202

Gutman, Yisrael, *The Jews of Warsaw*. Indiana University.

Hart, Kitty, *I am Alive*. Corgi Books.

Hersey, John, *The Wall*. Bantam (paperback), Modern Library hardcover.

Huberband, Rabbi Shimon, *Kidush Hashem*. Yeshiva University Press.

Kaufman, Michael T., *Mad Dreams, Saving Graces*. Random House.

Korczak, Janusz, *King Matt the First*. (Farrar, Straus, and Giroux.

Korczak, Janusz, *The Ghetto Years*. Ghetto Fighters House.

Krajewska, Monika, *Time of Stones*. Interpress-Warsaw.

Krall, Hannah, *Shielding the Flame*.

Kurzman, Dan, *The Bravest Battle: The 28 Days of the Warsaw Uprising*. Pinnacle Books.

Levi, Primo, *Moments of Reprieve*, Peguin

Levin, Nora, *The Holocaust: The Destruction of European Jewry*. Schocken.

Lifton, Betty Jean, *The King of Children—Biography of Janusz Korczak*, Farrar, Straus, and Giroux.

Marek, Bernard, *Warsaw Ghetto Uprising*.

Milosz, Czeslaw, *Campo di Fiori*.

Moczarski, Kazimierz, *Conversations with an Executioner*, Prentice-Hall.

Novich, Miriam, *Sobibor*. Holocaust Library.

Piotrowski, Stanislaw, *Hans Frank Diary*. P.W.N.-Warsaw.

Postal, Bernard, and Samuel Abramson, *The Traveler's Guide to Jewish Landmarks of Europe*. Fleet Press.

Ringelblum, Emanuel, *The Journal of Emanuel Ringelblum*. Schocken.

Ringelblum, Emanuel, *Polish-Jewish, Relations During the Second World War*. Yad Vashem.

Rings, Werner, *Life with the Enemy*. Doubleday.

Singer, Issac Bashevis, *Magician of Lublin*. Fawcett (paperback), Farrar, Straus, and Giroux (hardcover).
Trunk, Isaiah, *Jewish Responses to Nazi Persecution*. Stein & Day.
Uris, Leon, *Mila 18*. Bantam.
Weisel, Elie, *Night*. Avon.

Additional Bibliography

Most of the books are mentioned in Appendix IV. Theses additional books will add to your knowledge of Polish Jewry.

Rada Ochrony, *Pomnikow Lata Wojny, 1939-1945*
Scenes of Martyrdom and Fighting of Jews on the Polish Lands, 1939-1945
Przewodnik Po Upamietnionych Miejscach Walk i Meczenstwa
Carol H. Krinsky, *Synagogues of Europe*
Martin Gilbert, *Jewish History Atlas*
Martin Gilbert, *The Holocaust*
Emanuel Ringelblum, *Kronika Getta Warszawskiego*
Karol Estreicher, *Krakow*
Bernard Postal and Samuel H. Abrason, *The Traveller's Guide to Jewish Landmarks of Europe*
Josef Marszalek, *Majdanek*
Kazimierz Smolen, *Auschwitz*
Interpress, *Oswiecim*
Zwiazek Religijny, *Kaledaz Zydowski-Almanach*
Sport i Turystyka, *Maly Przewodnik po Polsce*
Lucjan Dobroszycki, *The Chronicle of the Lodz Ghetto, 1941-1944*
Muzeum Sztuki, *Cmentarz Zydowski w Lodzi*
Henryk Kroszczor and Henryk Zimler, *Cmentarz Zydowski w Warszawie*
Ryszard Wasita, *In The Land We Shared*
Kazimierz Smolen and Teresa Swioebocka, *Auschwitz, A Crime Against Mankind*
Simon Wiesenthal, *Every Day Remembrance Day*
Richard Yaffe and Abraham Davidson, *Nathan Rapoport Sculptures and Monuments*

APPENDIX V

Index of Locations

Other Cities of Jewish Interest

Bielawa
Czelno
Halich
Kalisz
Kisielice
Klodzko
Kolake

Kotno
Lesko
Lukow
Olsztyn
Orle
Wegrow

Pronunciation of Polish Towns:

Bialystok = Biyaleestock
Krakow = Krakoov
Lodz = Woodge
Lublin = Loobleen
Majdanek = Maydaneck
Oswiecim = Oshweetzeem
Rzeszow = Zheshoov
Treblinka = Trebleenka
Warszawa = Varshava